Science and Technology

Science and Technology

Inside Ancient China

JAMES STRAPP

Sharpe Focus

an imprint of M.E. Sharpe, Inc.

First edition for the United States, its territories and dependencies,
Canada, Mexico, and Australia, published in 2009

Sharpe Focus
An imprint of M.E. Sharpe, Inc.
80 Business Park Drive
Armonk, NY 10504

www.sharpe-focus.com

Library of Congress Cataloging-in-Publication Data

Strapp, James.
  Science and technology / James Strapp.
    p. cm. -- (Inside ancient China)
  Includes bibliographical references and index.
  ISBN 978-0-7656-8169-0 (hardcover : alk. paper)
  1. Science--China--History--To 1500. 2. Technology--China--History--To
1500. 3. Science and civilization. 4. Technology and civilization. I.
Title.

  Q127.C5S85 2009
  609.31--dc22

                        2008031168

Editorial and design by Amber Books Ltd
Project Editor: James Bennett
Consultant Editor: Susan Whitfield
Copy Editor: Constance Novis
Picture Research: Terry Forshaw, Natascha Spargo
Design: Joe Conneally

Cover Design: Jesse M. Sanchez, M.E. Sharpe, Inc.

Printed in Malaysia

9 8 7 6 5 4 3 2 1

ABOUT THE AUTHOR
James Strapp holds a BA Honors degree in Chinese from SOAS, University of London, which included special papers in
pre-Han archaeology and early Buddhist sculpture. He currently works at the British Museum as Schools and Young
Audiences Education Officer on the museum's First Emperor exhibition. He also runs two after-school Chinese clubs at
London schools, and in his spare time acts as an expert guide on Voyages Jules Verne vacations to China.

Contents

Introduction

China is the world's oldest continuous civilization, originating in the plains and valleys of the Yellow and Yangtze rivers more than six thousand years ago. In the third century B.C.E., the separate kingdoms of China were united to form an empire. Over the centuries China was ruled by a series of ruling houses, or families, known as dynasties. The empire was governed by an emperor, who was advised by highly educated scholars and who commanded a strong army. No dynasty lasted for more than a few hundred years and several were founded by invaders, such as the Mongol Yuan Dynasty and the Manchu Qing Dynasty. Successive dynasties expanded Chinese territory, until the empire extended into the northern steppes, the western deserts, and the southern tropics, reaching the extent of the China we know today.

China was not always united. Often the fall of dynasties resulted in long periods where different groups competed for power. Dynasties sometimes overlapped, each controlling a part of China. Throughout all these periods, the rulers retained classical Chinese as the official language, and many dynasties saw great cultural and technological developments. Through ancient trade routes and political missions, Chinese culture reached the rest of Asia, Europe, and Africa. Chinese technologies— including the compass, paper, gunpowder, and printing—had a profound effect on civilization throughout Eurasia. China was, in turn, greatly influenced by its neighbors, resulting in a diverse and complex civilization.

Science and Technology

Inventions often arise from necessity and, with its constant need to equip an army to repel powerful invaders and to feed its rising population, ancient China made great contributions to military and agricultural technologies, including gunpowder, the compass, the iron plow, the horse harness, the blast furnace, the crossbow, the wheelbarrow, and the water wheel. The ancient Chinese were at the forefront of astrological science with the world's earliest manuscript star chart. Paper and printing also assisted the Chinese bureaucracy in their rule, but were also used much more widely. And, as in all societies, Chinese people made other advances to improve their everyday lives, including a complex system of medicine that is still widely used today.

This map shows the major present-day and ancient cities and regions mentioned in this book, along with the eastern part of the Silk Road and the Grand Canal.

Samarka

The Main Dynasties of China

Shang   c. 1600–c. 1050 B.C.E.
Zhou   c. 1050–221 B.C.E.

The Zhou Dynasty can be divided into:
    Western Zhou   1050–771 B.C.E.
    Eastern Zhou   770–221 B.C.E.

The Eastern Zhou Dynasty can also be divided into the following periods:
    Spring and Autumn Period   770–476 B.C.E.
    Warring States Period   475–221 B.C.E.

Qin   221–206 B.C.E.
Han   206 B.C.E.–220 C.E.

From 221 C.E. to 589 C.E., different regions of China were ruled by several different dynasties and emperors in a period of disunity.

Sui   589–618 C.E.
Tang   618–907 C.E.

There was another period of disunity between the Tang and Song dynasties.

Song   960–1279 C.E.
Yuan   1279–1368 C.E.
Ming   1368–1644 C.E.
Qing   1644–1911 C.E.

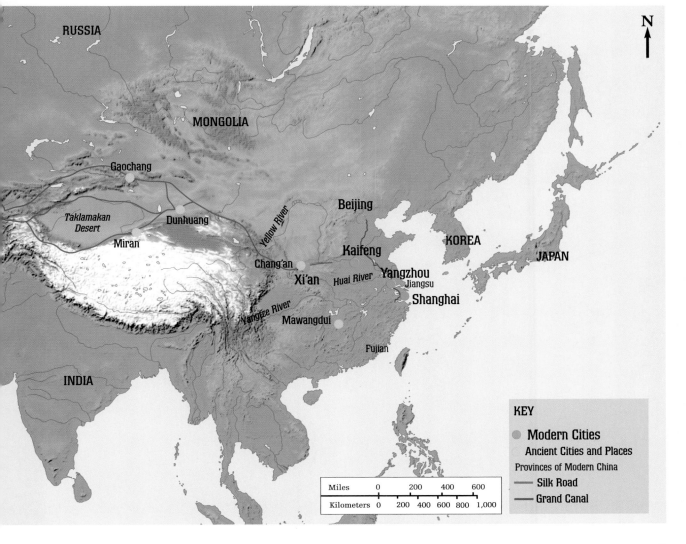

斗二度於辰在丑七度於辰在丑為星記者言統已萬物之終也

之分也

天柱

南

天皇

天牀

尾

北極

天棓

天槍

三公

太陽首

相

天理

勢

天安平

文昌

戊

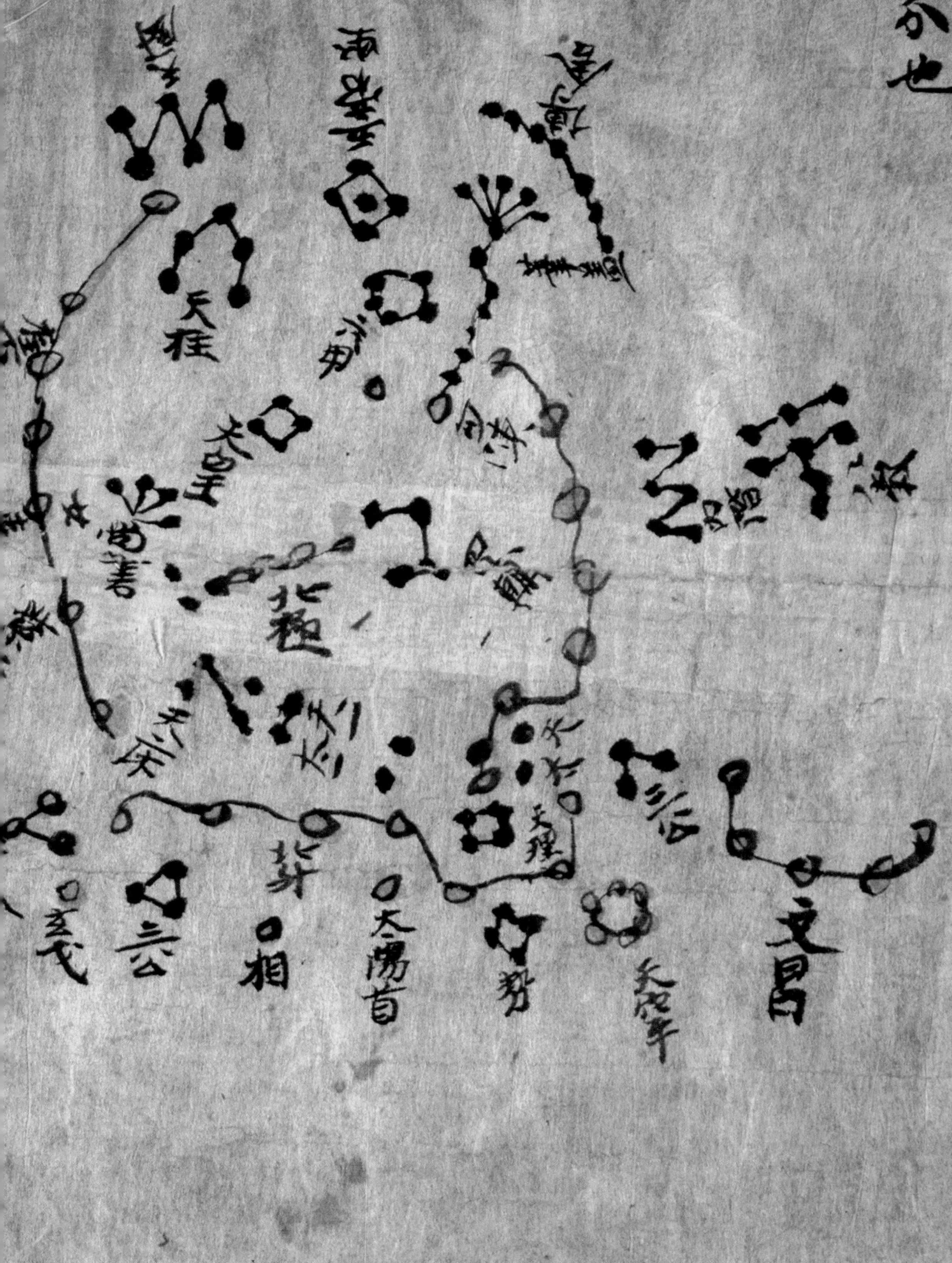

Chapter One

Finding the Way

The ancient Chinese needed to navigate across the vast area of China itself, as well as to other countries and continents. With the help of the compass, long-distance travel became much more manageable. Inside the country, building canals and waterways helped the emperors transport grain to feed their people, wood to build their palaces, and money to pay for it all. The ancient Chinese were able to travel greater and greater distances by sea as they improved their map-making skills and made advances in shipbuilding.

First Compasses

Many discoveries are made and then forgotten before, by chance, their actual full use is realized. An ancient Chinese book, *The Book of the Devil Valley Master*, talks about the power of a certain stone to attract iron and to show directions. The book says, "The lodestone makes iron come or it attracts it," and, "When the people of Cheng go out to collect jade, they take a south-pointer with them so as not to lose their way." The stone they were using is now known to be magnetite, a type of iron that is sometimes found to be naturally magnetized, when it is known as a lodestone. At some time not long after the book was written it seems that scientists and fortune-tellers began to investigate the magnetic properties of lodestones more closely. It is possible that it was First Emperor Qin (*Chin*) (259–210 B.C.E.), who ruled from 221–210 B.C.E., who ordered that this discovery be used seriously.

The ancient Chinese recognized different constellations from those we identify in the West. This is part of the earliest known map of the stars, found in the caves at Dunhuang, which dates from the seventh or eighth century C.E.

By the second half of the Han Dynasty (206 B.C.E.–220 C.E.), fortune-tellers were using specially designed boards to make predictions using lodestones. In the center of these boards they placed a magnetic pointer made from a piece of lodestone shaped like a spoon. The fortune-tellers of this time used a combination of the science of astronomy and mystic elements, including astrology, to tell the future, and it is not at all clear whether the actual direction their magnetic pointers showed was more important than the fact that it always pointed the same way. It is interesting to note that in the West we talk about a compass pointing to north, but in China people have always concentrated on the other end of the pointer, meaning that compasses always showed the direction of south. The shape of the pointer was meant to reflect the shape of the constellation that we call the Big Dipper. The ancient Chinese called this constellation *Bei Dou*, meaning Northern Dipper or Northern Ladle. We have no evidence that the Han Dynasty Chinese had discovered the secret of making objects magnetic. Instead they had to rely on finding natural lodestones, which added to the mystery of the process.

Fortune-tellers in the Han Dynasty used boards with a magnetic spoon-pointer such as this. The characters describe the eight points of the compass, along with symbols from the *Yijing* (Classic of Changes), an ancient manual of divination.

The South-Pointing Carriage

In addition to magnetic pointing devices, the story of another navigation device runs through Chinese history from legend into fact. This is the *Zhi Nan Che* (south-pointing carriage). In Chinese mythology, Huang Di (whose name means Yellow Emperor), who was said to be the founder of the Chinese nation, fought a battle with an enemy called Chi You. Chi You summoned up a magic fog to confuse the enemy, and Huang Di used his south-pointing carriage to show his army the way out.

A book written in the sixth century C.E., the *Songshu* (The History of the Song) tells us more about this machine. It is clear not only that it did exist, but also that it worked by mechanical means, rather than magnetism. Its secrets seem to have been lost and rediscovered several times between the third century B.C.E. and the eighth century C.E. The south-pointing carriage worked through a complicated system of gears, which meant that whichever way the chariot was turned, the figure standing in it always pointed south. It was used both for imperial ceremonies and for military purposes. The *Songshu* also mentions a south-pointing ship, though nothing more is known of this invention. In the early twelfth century C.E. an engineer called Wu Deren built a south-pointing carriage that also had an odometer, an instrument for measuring the distance the vehicle had traveled.

The only information we have about the south-pointing carriage comes from books, because none of the machines have survived to the present day. This is an artist's impression.

The standing figure faced south whichever way the chariot turned.

The carriage used a sophisticated set of cogs and gears.

Sturdy wheels meant that the carriage could be taken on military campaigns.

The Science of Magnetizing Iron

Although the history of the development of the magnetic compass in China is still not clear, clues can be found in historical sources. At some point, probably in the eighth or ninth century C.E., Chinese scientists discovered that instead of relying only on naturally magnetic lodestones, they could use them to magnetize pieces of iron. However, the charge was not very strong and did not last long. The next discovery was that iron heated until it was red hot, and then allowed to cool while aligned in a north–south direction, itself became magnetic. This meant that the ancient Chinese could now make fine pointers to be used in direction-finding devices.

Historians believe that the ancient Chinese used what is called a "wet" compass in which a needle, shaped like a fish, floated on water, although there are some descriptions of needles suspended on silk thread. When not in use, the needle was kept in a tightly sealed box with a lodestone in its base to maintain the magnetic charge. When it was needed it was taken out and floated on a basin of water in a place sheltered from the wind.

The first description of a compass, with a needle in the shape of a fish, comes from a military manual written in 1044 C.E. by Zheng Gongliang. It was entitled the *Compendium of Important Military Techniques*, and it also mentions the south-pointing carriage:

When troops encountered gloomy weather or dark nights, and the directions of space could not be distinguished, they let an old horse go on before to lead them, or else they made use of the south-pointing carriage or the south-pointing fish to identify the directions. Now the carriage method has not been handed down, but in the fish method a thin leaf of iron is cut into the shape of a fish two inches long and half an inch broad, having a pointed head and tail. This is then heated in a charcoal fire, and when it has become thoroughly red-hot, it is taken out by the head with iron tongs and placed so that its tail points due north. In this position it is quenched with water in a basin, so that its tail is submerged for several tenths of an inch. It is then kept in a tightly closed box. To use it, a small bowl filled with water is set up in a windless place, and the fish is laid as flat as possible on the water surface so that it floats, whereupon its head will point south.

Master Mapmakers

Books that have survived from the Han Dynasty (206 B.C.E.–220 C.E.) tell us that government departments of the time were using maps, which were considered to be very valuable items. Two men from around this same time made enormous contributions to the science of mapmaking in China. The first was Zhang Heng (*Jang-hung*) (78–139 C.E.), a famous scholar and inventor. He began to develop the idea of using grids and scales to make more accurate

By the sixteenth century, sophisticated equipment such as this combination compass and sundial was available. This instrument was used to ensure that buildings were positioned in the most auspicious place and alignment—a practice known as *Feng Shui*.

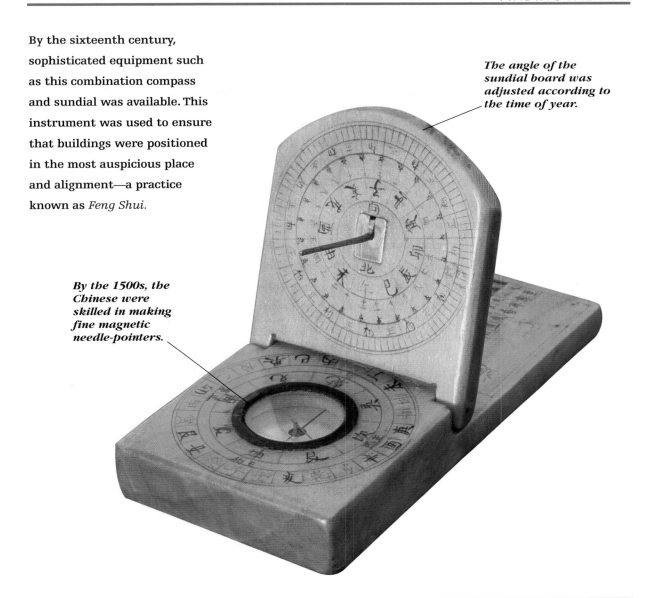

The angle of the sundial board was adjusted according to the time of year.

By the 1500s, the Chinese were skilled in making fine magnetic needle-pointers.

Shen Kuo

Early Chinese compasses became more accurate thanks to the observations made by a great scientist of the Northern Song Dynasty (960–1127 C.E.) named Shen Kuo. He discovered and calculated the difference between "true" north and magnetic north. The earliest known navigational compasses of the eleventh century show this knowledge in their markings, and twelfth-century manuscripts show that the Chinese were using a compass for accurate sea navigation when neither sun nor stars were visible. According to a written record from 1124 C.E. by Xu Jing (*Shoo-jing*), "During the night it is often not possible to stop because of wind or current drift, so the pilot has to steer by the stars and the Great Bear. If the night is overcast then he uses the south-pointing floating needle to determine south and north."

Maps from Ancient Times

Fictional stories and historical clues tell us a lot about maps and mapmaking in ancient China. In one famous story an assassin attempts to kill the First Emperor Qin by hiding a knife in a rolled-up map. It is also recorded that a model of the world (as the ancient Chinese then knew it) was created on the floor of Qin's tomb chamber, with the rivers and oceans flowing in mercury. The earliest maps so far discovered, drawn in ink on blocks of wood, were found in a fourth-century B.C.E. tomb. The most famous early maps, however, are from an important Han Dynasty (206 B.C.E.–220 C.E.) tomb of the first half of the second century B.C.E. in Mawangdui, and these were written in ink on silk. Though they are not drawn to a scale, they do make notes of distances, and use symbols to represent different features in the landscape.

Archaeologists excavated a number of Han Dynasty tombs at Mawangdui in 1972. As well as real maps, they also discovered this amazing silk banner which shows a map of the spirit journey of Lady Dai after her death.

The whole top section depicts heaven. The red disc with a black bird is the symbol of the sun.

These two giant sea-serpents are in the underworld.

This silk banner has survived for more than 2,000 years—even the weighted silk tassels are intact.

maps. However, we also know that the man who made the biggest contribution to mapmaking did not consider Han Dynasty maps to be of very good quality or of much use. That man was Pei Xiu (*Pay-shee'oh*). He lived between 224 and 271 C.E., and was the Minister of Works for one of the emperors of the Jin Dynasty (265–420 C.E.), a short-lived dynasty that came after the Han Dynasty. Xiu made a study of all the existing maps of China at the time and came up with six "Principles of Mapmaking." Although these are too complex to explain in detail here, the guiding rule of Pei Xiu's principles was that that a map should give accurate information about distances. To achieve this he perfected the use of grids and graduated scale on his maps. He also developed new methods of showing elevation or height so that mountains and valleys could be more accurately represented.

Surviving Maps

Very few early maps from China have survived over time, but historical writings indicate just how highly the ancient Chinese regarded maps. As well as flat maps on silk and paper, army generals and commanders used three-dimensional models, or relief maps, to help plan their campaigns. Some of these maps are described as being carved from wood, but others were modeled in rice. The earliest reference to a relief map being used for military purposes is from the first century C.E., but a much earlier relief map was said to be in the tomb of First Emperor Qin (259–210 B.C.E.).

Over the following centuries, emperors ordered bigger and better maps to be made to enable them to understand and control their empire better. In the Tang Dynasty (618–907 C.E.) Emperor Dezong, who reigned from 779 to 805 C.E., commanded Jia Dan to produce a map of China and the desert lands to the west. The finished map, using a scale of roughly 1 inch to 100 *li* (the ancient Chinese unit of length equivalent to about one-third of a mile or half a kilometer) measured 30 feet by 33 feet (9 meters by 10 meters). Emperor Taizu (reigned 927–946 C.E.) of the Song Dynasty (960–1279 C.E.) ordered his Minister of Works to update all the known information and maps about all the provinces and territories in his empire. The completed work had more than 1,500 chapters. From the sixth century onward, mapmakers had also found a way of making sure their work survived the passage of time by carving in stone on large standing tablets called *stelae* (the plural of *stele*). The most famous of all the *stele* maps dates from the Song Dynasty and can still be seen in the modern city of Xi'an. It is known as the *Yu Ji Tu*, measures 3 feet by 3 feet (0.9 meters by 0.9 meters), uses a scale grid of 100 *li* per square, and shows all the territory of China, as well as Korea in the north and India in the south.

The Yangtze river on the *Yu Ji Tu* stele map is almost identical to its appearance on modern maps.

Steering Clear: The Ship's Rudder

Even with accurate maps and magnetic compasses none of the great sea journeys ever made by Europeans, Chinese, or anyone else would have been possible without the ship's rudder, another Chinese invention. The earliest ships of many cultures had steering devices in the form of a long

Zheng He: World Explorer?

During the Song Dynasty (960–1279 C.E.) the ancient Chinese learned to use compasses more accurately. When they combined this with their ability to produce accurate maps, the world began to open up to their traders and explorers. The most famous of all these explorers lived a little later, in the early fifteenth century C.E. His name was Zheng He (*Jeng-huh*). Zheng He himself was not ethnically Chinese. He came from a Muslim family from southern Asia. Both his father and his grandfather had traveled great distances in their lives. Zheng He became a trusted official of the Emperor Yongle (*Yong-luh*) (1360–1424 C.E.), who put him in command of the imperial fleet. For twenty-eight years between 1405 and 1433, Zheng He led seven expeditions to spread the influence of China across the oceans. In the course of those expeditions, sometimes leading a fleet with as many as 300 ships, he reached as far as modern Kenya on the eastern coast of Africa and the Arabian Peninsula. He took Chinese traders and settlers to such countries as India, Sri Lanka, Indonesia, Thailand, Vietnam, and Cambodia. It is known that these voyages were made possible by the existence of accurate maps from earlier times, but also that Zheng He himself brought back maps and information that were included in a master atlas, called the *Guang Yu Tu*, which was published in 1579.

It has been claimed that Zheng He sailed even further than Africa, and actually managed to circumnavigate the globe, reaching America before Magellan and Columbus. In 2006 a map was discovered in China that some people claim proves this. They believe that this map is an accurate copy, made in the eighteenth century, of a much earlier map made in 1418 after one of Zheng He's voyages. It shows all of Africa, Europe, North and South America, and even Australia with

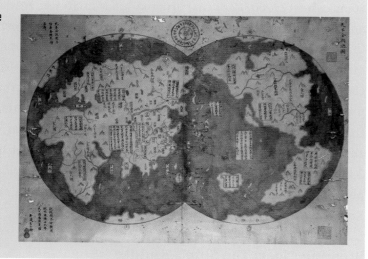

place names and descriptions of the people who lived there. The authenticity of this map and of the claims that the Chinese did indeed reach these distant lands has not finally been settled, but it does now seem unlikely that either is true.

Even if the Zheng He map is not genuine, we may yet be amazed by how far across the oceans early Chinese explorers reached.

200 B.C.E.			300 C.E.
Qin Dynasty 221–206 B.C.E.	Han Dynasty 206 B.C.E.–220 C.E.		Jin Dynasty 265–420 C.E.
First Emperor Qin 259–210 B.C.E.	Zhang Heng 78–139 C.E.	Pei Xiu 224–271 C.E.	

oar, but the idea of mounting a specially shaped board under the stern of the vessel was developed by the Chinese.

The first evidence we have of rudder design is in a pottery model of a ship buried in a first-century C.E. tomb during the Han Dynasty (206 B.C.E.–220 C.E.). Archaeologists can learn a great deal about all aspects of daily life from these models, and sometimes, as in this case, they provide the evidence for important inventions of ancient Chinese technologies.

The realistic modeling of this Han Dynasty pottery boat gives us a lot of information about ancient ship technology. Similar-looking boats are used on the waterways of China today.

The stern-mounted rudder revolutionized water transport.

Whole families lived and worked on boats such as these.

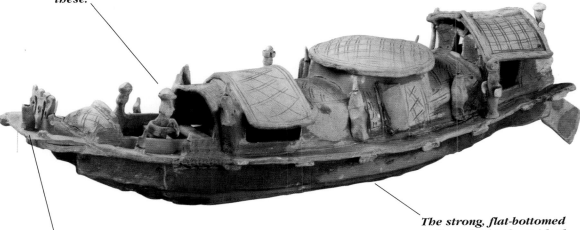

The boat has a Y-shaped anchor made of stone.

The strong, flat-bottomed hull made this boat ideal for use on China's rivers and canals.

		800 C.E.		1200 C.E.	
	Sui Dynasty 589–618 C.E.	Tang Dynasty 618–907 C.E.		Song Dynasty 960–1279 C.E.	
	Wendi 541–604 C.E.	Qiao Weiyo invents pound lock 984 C.E.	Shen Kuo 1031–1095 C.E.		Zheng He 1371–1433 C.E.

The model shows us that the ship's rudder was already an established piece of equipment at this time, so it must have been invented many years earlier. There is no way of knowing exactly when, and nothing is written in historical records about it. We can, however, see that the rudder was of a large size, and would have been mounted under the ship with ropes that could be used to draw it up if the ship went into shallow water where the rudder might be damaged.

The earliest evidence for the use of a rudder in Europe dates from the end of the twelfth century C.E., 1,100 years later. The Chinese further improved their rudder design over the centuries, changing the way it was mounted and also piercing the solid planks of wood with holes. Both these things made the rudder much easier and lighter to move through the water and made the task of steering easier and more accurate. Neither of these improvements was adopted in the West until the late nineteenth and early twentieth centuries.

Master Engineers: Canal Building

China is a country of great rivers, particularly the Yellow and the Yangtze rivers, and for many centuries the Chinese have been expert at using water and waterways for transportation and for power. As far back as the eighth century B.C.E. artificial waterways were built in north and central China both to help water crops and for military purposes. Depending on the weather and the season they were used either to flood or draw water away from an enemy's territory. The first transport canal was dug in the sixth and fifth centuries B.C.E. to connect two natural waterways, the Yellow River and the Huai River in central China. It was called the Hong Gou canal.

Once again, it was First Emperor Qin (259–210 B.C.E.) who saw effective ways in which canals could be used. Transportation, both on land and water, was of vital importance to him in keeping control of his new empire, and he built thousands of miles of roads and canals. The most famous of his canals is the one, still in use today, called *Ling Qu* (*Ling-choo*) (The Magic Canal). This was the first-ever transportation canal built following the natural contours, or features, of the land. It is only 20 miles (32 kilometers) long, but it too forms a link between two rivers, the Xiang River (*Shee'ang*) as it flows north and the Li River as it flows south. That link between the rivers meant that the First Emperor's ships and barges could then sail 1,250 miles (2,000 kilometers) on the Xiang and the Li carrying vital food and supplies from the south of the empire to the north.

The Grand Canal

Canals remained an important means of transportation from that time on. In the sixth century C.E. the first emperor of the Sui Dynasty (589–618 C.E.), Wendi (541–604 C.E.), and his son Yangdi (569–618 C.E.) started a huge new project of canal building. As well as restoring old canals, they

The Grand Canal in Suzhou is still a busy waterway today. As in ancient times, long convoys of heavily loaded barges pass by the houseboats of sailors and their families.

The Canal Builders

First Emperor Qin used hundreds of thousands of men as laborers, some of them convicts, others captured soldiers from the kingdoms he conquered, and other ordinary people forced to take their turn working for the Emperor. Building canals in those days was hard and dangerous work, and many of them would not have survived.

realized that it would be possible to join up existing waterways and build new sections where necessary to create one continuous route. When it was finished, it is said that more than five million people had worked on it. It linked six river systems and joined Hangzhou in the south with Beijing in the north. It is known as the Grand Canal, and to celebrate the opening, Emperor Yangdi led a 65-mile (105-kilometer) procession of boats to his capital at Yangzhou (*Yang-joe*). The Grand Canal continued to be the most important transportation route in China for the next thirteen centuries.

All manner of goods and materials were transported along the Grand Canal, including all the timber to build the Forbidden City in Beijing. This is a detail of a scroll map of the canal dating from the 1700s.

The Pound-Lock

The pound-lock is used worldwide on canals to move boats between stretches of water at two different levels. It has two sets of gates that shut the boat in so that the water level inside, and thus the boat, can be raised or lowered. Before the invention of the lock, the raising and lowering of boats was a dangerous business involving hauling boats with ropes up slopes or slipways and then letting them slide down the other side back into the water—a drop that often damaged or even sank the boats. This was obviously very dangerous, costly, and time-consuming. The pound-lock was invented in 984 C.E. by an Assistant Commissioner of Transport named Qiao Weiyo (*Chee'ow-way-you*), whose job it was to supervise the transportation of taxes.

When traveling between a lower and higher section of canal, a boat enters the lock through a pair of gates when the water level inside is at its lowest level.

With the lower gates closed, valves in the upper gates are opened to allow water to gradually enter the lock. The boat rises with the water.

When the water level inside the lock is the same as that in the upper section of canal, the gates can be opened and the boat can continue on its journey.

Chapter Two

The Story of Silk

Silk was one of the great discoveries—and great mysteries—of ancient China. Emperors kept its secrets from the outside world for thousands of years, and anyone who dared betray them was said to have been put to death. Silk was seen as a gift from the gods and had countless uses. Selling it brought untold wealth to China. The trade route for transporting silk across Central Asia, known as the Silk Road, brought with it new ideas, new art, and new religions into ancient China.

Mythical Origins of Silk

According to Chinese legend, silk was discovered by one of the wives of the mythological Huang Di (whose name means Yellow Emperor). Her name was Leizu or Xi Lingshi and, according to the tale, as she was sitting drinking tea in a grove of mulberry trees about 5,000 years ago, she saw cocoons of a certain type of moth hanging among the branches of the trees. She gathered some to study them more closely. As she was examining them, one of them dropped into the cup of tea she was drinking. When she fished the cocoon out of her cup, she noticed that as it had got wet, it had begun to unravel very slightly. She took the loose end of the thread that had appeared and slowly began to pull it out. To her amazement she kept pulling and pulling as though it would go on forever. She could tell how strong and soft the thread was, and the idea came to her of weaving it into cloth. She was so excited she hurried back to tell her husband. He listened carefully and then told her that she must study the life of the moth that produced these cocoons so that she and her maidservants could learn to cultivate them. From that point on, Leizu was known as the patron goddess of silk.

From the earliest times, women managed all stages of silk production in China. The most skillful part was weaving complex patterns using looms, as shown in this detail from a Ming Dynasty vase.

Where Silk Comes From

The thread used to make cultivated silk comes from the cocoon of the silk moth, *Bombyx mori*. Legends aside, the first evidence that people had learned its secrets is the discovery of a cocoon that had been cut in half with a knife at a site in northern China that dates back to sometime around 3000 B.C.E. Farther south, in Zhejiang (*Juh-jee'ang*) province, small fragments of silk thread and even of woven silk material have been found that are about the same age. It is likely that silk culture goes back even further than this because a silkworm pattern is very a common decoration on pottery that may be as much as 2,000 years older. Very ancient fragments of wood have also been identified as parts of early silk-weaving frames or looms.

The characters for silk, silkworm, silk thread, and mulberry tree are all found in the earliest form of Chinese writing. These were the inscriptions scratched onto ox bones and tortoiseshell

The silkworm is tiny when it first hatches from its egg, but in just over 40 days it increases almost 10,000 times in weight before it starts to spin its cocoon.

The Qing Dynasty emperors and their court wore magnificent woven silk robes that showed their rank. This style of robe is called a *Jifu*, which means "auspicious coat."

The high, round collar is typical of Qing court dress.

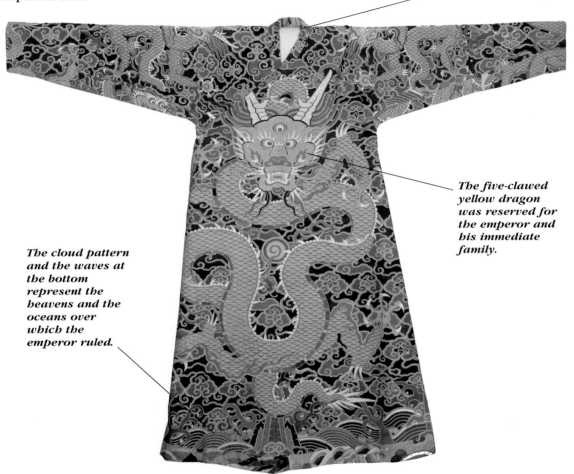

The five-clawed yellow dragon was reserved for the emperor and his immediate family.

The cloud pattern and the waves at the bottom represent the heavens and the oceans over which the emperor ruled.

used to tell the future in the Bronze Age Shang Dynasty (c. 1600–1050 B.C.E.). It is clear that from that time on, all the basics of silk production were well known to the Chinese and they were quickly able to produce textiles of the finest quality.

From the beginning silk was recognized as being very special. Indeed, it does have almost magical properties. Unlike other yarns such as wool and flax, it is produced by an insect; it is very light but very strong; and when made into cloth it is cool in the summer and warm in the winter. For many centuries only the emperors and the most noble of families used silk. They made it into robes and dresses, but it was also used for decorations, for paintings, banners, and wall hangings. Around the fifth century B.C.E. important documents began to be written on silk.

Mawangdui: A Treasure House of Silk

The most important archaeological discovery of ancient silk use was made at a place called Mawangdui in Hunan province. In 1972 three tombs of the early Han Dynasty (206 B.C.E.–220 C.E.) were discovered there. They contained the burials of the Marquis of Dai, his wife, and his son. The tombs, particularly that of the Lady Dai, were in an amazing state of preservation. Her body had been naturally mummified so scientists were able to reconstruct exactly how she had looked, how she died, and even what she had eaten for her last meal. The emperor of that time had decreed that no precious objects made of gold or jade should be placed in tombs, so instead, what the archaeologists found was treasure of a different kind. All the Lady's personal possessions—cosmetics sets, cups, bowls, and chopsticks made out of lacquer—were there. Her body was wrapped in many layers of finest silk cloth and on top was laid a long T-shaped

Harvesting Silk Thread

The process of cultivating and making silk, called sericulture, has changed very little over the centuries. The silkworm feeds only on the leaves of particular types of mulberry tree, and no successful substitute for this food has ever been found. A single moth lays 300–400 eggs at a time, each about the size of a pinhead. The eggs hatch after ten days and the larva are about half an inch (1.25 centimeters) long. They are carefully protected in specially made trays stacked one on top of another, and the temperature is closely watched. They are fed huge quantities of mulberry leaves for the next 35 days until they are many thousands of times heavier than when they hatched. When they reach a certain size they naturally begin to spin themselves cocoons from spinnerets in their heads. It takes them two to four days to finish the cocoon, which is made of a single thread up to 3,000 feet (915 meters) long. If left alone, the pupae inside the cocoon begin to give off a chemical that "melts" the cocoon so it can escape when it becomes a moth. A few are left to do this so that there will be a new generation of moths to lay eggs, but most are killed inside the cocoon at this point using heat. Just as in the legend of Leizu, the cocoons must then be soaked in hot water to loosen the end of the thread. The cocoon is unraveled into one long continuous strand and several of these are then twisted together to make a thread strong enough to use for weaving and embroidery.

Even when they are safely in their cocoons, the silkworms have to be very closely watched. Silk-workers have to choose just the right moment to harvest the silk.

silk banner painted with the story of the journey the Lady Dai made to heaven after her death. Many other documents written on silk were also found in this tomb and that of the young prince. They include an illustration of a set of exercises that seem to be the forerunner of *Taiqiquan (T'ai Ch'i)*, a description of the movements of the planets and comets, some medical texts, and copies of some important books of philosophy. Altogether, the tombs at Mawangdui are one of the most important archaeological finds in all China, and they are certainly also the most complete source of information about the use of silk in early times.

Books on Silk

Two of the ancient classics of Chinese history, the *Shujing* (Classic of History) and the *Liji* (Classic of Rites) give us a lot of information about silk cultivation in early times. By the fifth century B.C.E. at least six provinces of China were dedicated to silk production, and in those provinces the women of every household would spend six months of the year devoted to making silk. Silk production was always seen as women's work and every year the wife of the emperor would hold a special ceremony to mark the beginning of the silk season.

Beginnings of the Silk Trade

From the earliest times, silk was of huge importance to the ancient Chinese. It began as a magical material to be used only by the most important in the land, but gradually its use widened. The ancient Chinese quickly found that this amazing material could be used for other things apart from clothes and decorations, or for writing or painting on. Its strength meant that it was ideal for strings for musical instruments, bowstrings, cords of all kinds, and even fishing line. In fact, it was so valuable that when First Emperor Qin (259–210 B.C.E.) unified the empire in 221 B.C.E. and standardized all weights, measures, and currency across China, he made a length of silk cloth one of the forms of money. From the Han Dynasty (206 B.C.E.–220 C.E.), silk was used by farmers to pay tax, and by the emperor to pay his officials.

For more than 3,000 years the Chinese managed to keep the secret of silk manufacture away from all foreigners. The Romans, for example, believed it grew on trees. This did not mean that the material itself did not travel out of China, just that no other people knew where it came from or how it was made.

It was the nomadic tribesmen of the steppes northwest of China who first began to trade with the Chinese for significant amounts of silk, starting in the sixth century B.C.E. Some of their tombs have been found in Siberia, perfectly preserved by frost, and inside them are magnificently embroidered silk cloths and saddle fittings. The ancient Greeks fought with these nomadic people in the west of their huge territories, and that is how they came into contact with silk. All they knew was that it came from a people they called the Seres who lived in a country far away to the east.

Silk production was always a family business. In this illustration from a Qing Dynasty book we can see a woman arranging racks of cocoons on the veranda of the family home.

Silk began reaching Rome in small quantities at the beginning of the first century B.C.E., but the trade grew quickly once the Romans had conquered Egypt and opened up trade with the East. Silk was so expensive in Imperial Rome, and such a highly desired luxury item, that the trade in silk was in danger of ruining the economy.

The Silk Road

People who have heard of the Silk Road (also referred to as the Silk Route) sometimes think it was some kind of highway specially built for the silk trade. In fact it is not one single road nor was it only silk that was carried along it. By the second century C.E., more and more traders from Central Asia were beginning to make regular journeys to trade along the route across vast distances between China and the shores of the Mediterranean Sea, though they did not travel the entire route. They were carrying all manner of goods, including silk, gold, silver, precious stones, rare spices, and exotic fruits; anything, in fact, that could be sold at a profit. However, the most valuable and remarkable thing they traded was, without a doubt, silk.

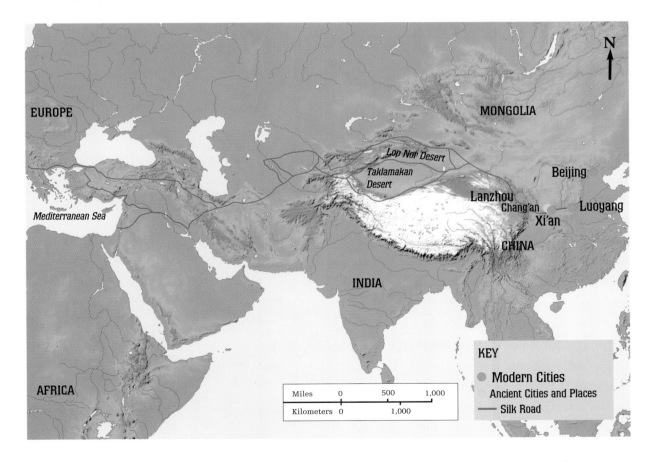

This map shows the major routes of the silk merchants who traded between the ancient Chinese cities of Luoyang and Chang'an and the Mediterranean Sea, 5,000 miles (8,000 km) away.

Traveling in Stages

The Silk Road covered a vast distance from end to end, almost 5,000 miles (8,000 kilometers). Treacherous weather conditions and attacks by nomads and bandits made it very dangerous. Therefore, goods were carried along the Silk Road in stages. One merchant would carry his wares as far as one of the many market towns and cities that grew up along the route, where he would sell them to another merchant who would carry them farther on and do the same thing. So in the end it was probably only very small quantities of silk that actually reached the shores of the Mediterranean, and by the time it got there it had increased many times in value.

Perils of the Silk Road

The center of silk production in China for many centuries has been the city of Suzhou in Jiangsu province. However, traditionally the route was seen as beginning and ending in the city of Chang'an, which is now called Xi'an, in Shaanxi (*Shaarn-shee*) province. The route out of China from Chang'an was not an easy one, and merchants who wished to make their fortune in the silk trade had to face many dangers. Hostile nomadic tribes and bandits were a constant threat, but worst of all were the deserts they had to cross. In China's most famous desert, the Gobi, temperatures can range from 122°F (50°C) in the summer to -40°F (-40°C) in the winter, but this was not the worst desert that travelers faced. West of the Gobi is a place called the Taklamakan. It is the second-largest shifting-sand desert in the world. In general the Taklamakan was

Bactrian camels like these were the main means of transport along the eastern part of the Silk Road. They are standing on the edge of the treacherous Taklamakan desert.

The filament from a cocoon can be up to half a mile in length, but several have to be spun together to make a thread for weaving. This painting of a woman with a spinning wheel dates from the Song Dynasty.

considered too dangerous to cross, so the Silk Road split in two going to the north and the south of it. Even this was difficult because high mountains surround the desert. Travelers on the Silk Road would stop at the many oasis towns bordering the desert. Some of these, such as Miran and Gaochang, were buried under its moving dunes and were lost for centuries until modern archaeologists uncovered their ruins.

To protect the trade that came in and out of China along the Silk Road, the emperors of the Han Dynasty (206 B.C.E.–220 C.E.) set up a special area of local government to control the region around the Taklamakan, and even built extensions to the Great Wall of China to try to ward off fierce nomad tribes such as the Xiongnu. Even so, the route remained very dangerous and often fell out of the control of the Chinese authorities.

Buddhism Reaches China

The Silk Road did not just bring valuable goods to many people but it also carried new ideas. One branch of the route traveled west across Central Asia toward Europe. However, another part of it branched south into modern-day Afghanistan, Pakistan, and northern India. The *Houhan Shu* (The Official History of the Later Han) tells this story of the dream of the Han Emperor Ming (28–75 C.E.):

The Tang Dynasty capital Chang'an
was the beginning of the Silk Road.
The Tang Emperor Gaozong ordered
the building of the Great Wild
Goose Pagoda to house Buddhist
scriptures brought back from India
by Xuanzang.

There is a current tradition that Emperor Ming dreamed that he saw a tall, golden man the top of whose head was glowing. He questioned his group of advisors and one of them said: "In the West there is a god called Buddha. His body is sixteen chi high [12 feet or 3.7 meters], *and is the color of true gold." The Emperor, to discover the true doctrine, sent an envoy to Tianzhu* (Tea'en-joo) [northwest India] *to inquire about the Buddha's doctrine, after which paintings and statues* [of the Buddha] *appeared in the Middle Kingdom* [China].

It is also recorded that as a result of this dream Emperor Ming ordered the building of the first Buddhist temple in China. How much of this is true is not known, but it is certain that from around this time onward Buddhist missionaries began to travel into China along the Silk Road from northern India, bringing with them both scriptures and religious art. The most famous of all Buddhist travelers was in fact a Chinese monk, Xuanzang of the Tang Dynasty (618–907 C.E.). He traveled from Chang'an to India to collect scriptures, which he brought back and translated into Chinese. In legend, one of his helpers on the journey was the Monkey God, who is still a favorite character in Chinese stories, opera, and television.

Silk and Status

Even though the custom of wearing silk spread beyond the imperial court and into the higher levels of society, certain colors and types of silk robes remained reserved for use only by court and government officials. This was especially true of the last two imperial dynasties, the Ming (1368–1644 C.E.) and the Qing (1644–1911 C.E.). The Qing rulers, who were actually foreign invaders from the northeast, generally adopted the Ming style of court robes with a few changes that came from their traditional dress. Many fine examples of court dress from this time still survive. Officials at the Qing court could be recognized by the color of their robes and the shape and design of the large embroidered insignia on them. High officials and low-ranking princes wore dark blue, blue, or brown, but only the very top members of the emperor's family could wear yellow, with different shades according to their importance. One shade of yellow was reserved for the emperor himself, and only he could wear embroidery showing a dragon with five claws on each foot.

From the very beginning, silk was appreciated as a very special material. Both legend and very early historical documents record that at first only the emperor and his family were allowed to wear it. For thousands of years, the common people of China were forbidden to wear silk, and could even be executed if they disobeyed. Silk was so precious that it was used as currency with a value greater than gold. It is recorded that in the Song Dynasty (960–1279 C.E.) the emperors paid out more than 500,000 bales of silk every year to buy peace with the nomadic kingdoms on their northern borders. As the rest of the world discovered the wonders of silk, its value increased many times and it brought great wealth into China along the Silk Road.

Chang'an and the Tang Dynasty

During the Tang Dynasty (618–907 C.E.) the use of the Silk Road was at its height. The Tang capital of Chang'an was almost certainly one of the largest cities in the world, with a population of over one million people. It must have been a spectacular place, with camel trains constantly entering and leaving the city. There were two huge market places in the east and the west. In the western market foreign merchants traded goods from all across the known world. A great deal about what Chang'an looked like is recorded in books written at the time, and there is an even clearer idea of what the trading caravans looked like from a more unusual source.

The custom of burying pottery models in tombs continued in the Tang Dynasty, and all around Chang'an there were factories producing magnificent glazed pottery figures for the tombs of the royal family and the court nobles. The finest of all these models, many of which have survived to this day, are those of camels and horses. The camel models represented the camels of the Silk Road. They were placed in the tombs to show what kind of luxury the dead person was used to in life and expected after death. Often the camels had human figures on them or standing beside them, and from these models we can see all the different nationalities of merchant who traded on the Silk Road and came to Chang'an to make their fortunes.

Merchants of many different nationalities traveled along the Silk Road. Many of them are depicted in the magnificent glazed pottery figures produced for burial in Tang Dynasty tombs.

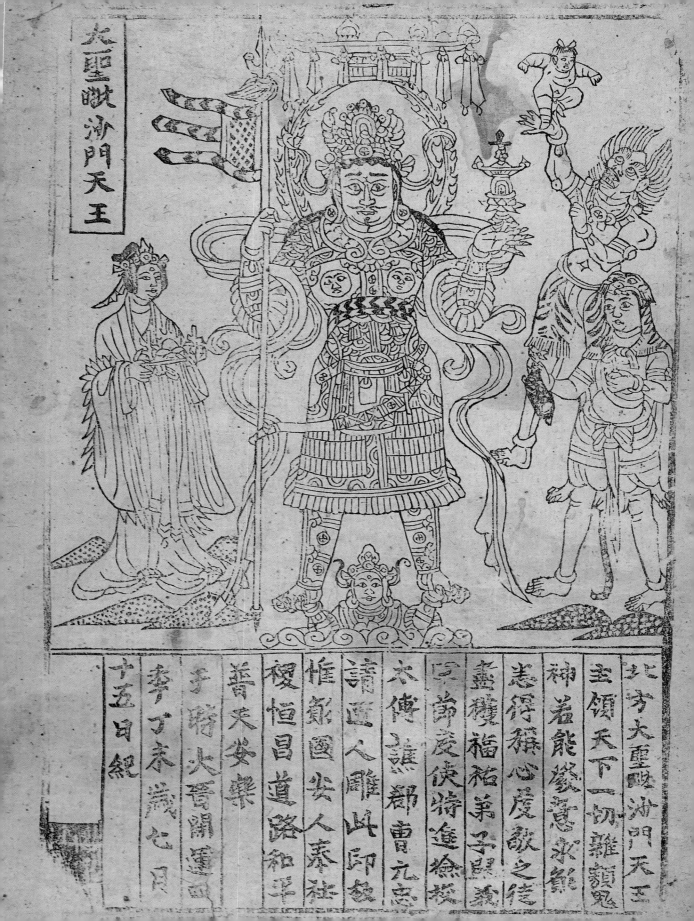

太聖毗沙門天王

北方大聖毗沙門天王
主領天下一切離顧鬼
神若能燃意求能
患得稱心慶歡之德
盡樓福祐弟子諷教
民節度使特進徐敬
太傅譙郡曹元忠
諷匠人雕此即款
惟願國安人泰社
稷恒昌道路和平
普天安樂
手眸火晉開運四
李丁未歲九月
十五日紀

Chapter Three

Paper

Paper may be the most important invention to come out of China. Cai Lun, the man credited with making the first writing paper, revolutionized the recording and distribution of information. Paper made it possible for the emperors to spread their laws across the country and organize their governments more efficiently; writers, philosophers, and historians could record their thoughts and ideas for others to share; and, with the invention of paper money, it even became as valuable as gold.

The earliest Chinese writing is not found on paper, but on bone, bronze, and pottery. During the Shang Dynasty, emperors seeking to know the future would scratch questions and receive answers on ox and tortoise bones. Metalworkers making ritual bronze vessels for kings and nobles cast inscriptions on them to record whom they were made for and when they were used. The earliest examples of writing on plant material that have been discovered date from the fifth century B.C.E. Bamboo was split and scraped to form long strips, which could be threaded together to form rough sheets for writing on. Sometimes wood was also used. The ink could be scraped off and the strips used again. Some of the terracotta figures discovered around the tomb of First Emperor Qin (259–210 B.C.E.) show officials with a small knife and sharpening

The King of Dunhuang commissioned this Buddhist woodblock print in 947 C.E. It is one of the earliest dated examples of printing and shows Vaisravana, the Guardian King of the North.

The kings of the Shang Dynasty had priests who used bone to predict the future. Some of the earliest Chinese writing is found on bones such as this.

The priests read the pattern of cracks that were made with a heated needle.

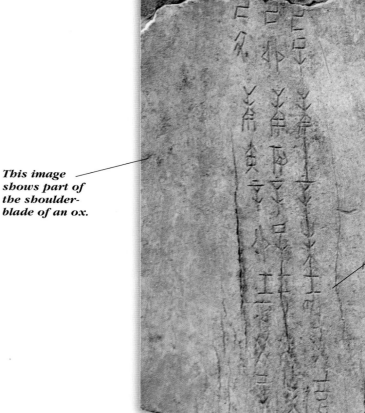

This image shows part of the shoulder-blade of an ox.

This ancient style of character is called Oracle Bone Script.

More than 100,000 oracle bones have been excavated, telling us a lot about Bronze Age China.

These fragments of paper with characters on them were found in Gansu province in the north-west of China. It is some of the earliest writing paper made from plant fiber.

stone on their belts, which were used for this purpose. These bamboo or wood strips continued to be used after the discovery of paper. Silk was also used for very special documents but was much too expensive and precious to be a general-purpose writing material.

Ancient Paper

The oldest paper discovered in China is from a Han Dynasty (206 B.C.E.–220 C.E.) tomb near Xi'an in Shaanxi province, where the Han had their imperial capital. It dates from between 140 and 87 B.C.E. Chapter Two describes a tomb of almost the same date at Mawangdui where painted silk documents and paintings were discovered. However, the paper in the Xi'an tomb was not used for writing material because it was much too rough and coarse. Instead, it was used as wrapping paper for some of the precious objects that were buried in the tomb. Archaeologists can tell, however, that it was made in the same way as writing paper: fibers from the hemp plant were pounded and soaked in water to form a pulp that could be spread out and dried. The earliest paper with writing on it was found on the Silk Road in the ruins of a watchtower from around 110 C.E. It is likely that paper for writing on was in use before this date because the document was not of special importance, indicating that paper by this time was common enough to be used for fairly ordinary official purposes.

The "Invention" of Paper

Despite the earlier history described above, tradition has it that the inventor of paper was a man called Cai Lun. It is not known when he was born, but he died in 121 C.E. He was an official in the court of the Emperor He (79–105 C.E.) who ruled from 89 to 105 C.E. during the Han Dynasty (206 B.C.E.–220 C.E.) In his work as a senior secretary, he would have had to deal with many documents every day. However, at that time official documents were still being written on bamboo strips, which were very heavy when many of them were bound together. It seems that Cai Lun had an inspiration. He realized that although the paper of the time, made from hemp, was not good enough for writing on, if he could refine it and make it smoother, stronger, and lighter, then it would be ideal for all kinds of official use. To achieve this he used a combination of the bark of trees, remnants of hemp, rags of cloth, and fishing nets. Soon this form of papermaking was widely used. Cai Lun did not leave any record of his invention himself, so it cannot be confirmed where he got the ideas from, but the materials he chose are not as strange as they may sound because rough paper had been made out of hemp for hundreds of years. The bark of trees, particularly a certain type of mulberry tree, had been used to make clothes and hats from as early as the sixth century B.C.E. Fishing nets would have been made from similar natural plant materials. Mixing in rags of cloth was probably an inspiration to try to create a type of paper with a texture as fine as woven cloth.

One System of Writing

More than 300 years before Cai Lun, First Emperor Qin (259–210 B.C.E.) gave an order that many historians believe was responsible more than anything else for the survival and

success of Chinese civilization. He wanted to strengthen the union of the ancient Chinese kingdoms by insisting that the whole country no longer use the different writing systems of the old kingdoms, but should all use one script. Cai Lun's "invention" of paper was the second vital stage of this. Not only could any written material—laws, literature, philosophy, or religion—be read and understood anywhere in the land, but it could also easily be copied and carried there on paper. The Han Dynasty (206 B.C.E.–220 C.E.), and those that came after it found it much easier to run the country using paper. The Chinese managed to keep the

Cai Lun's "invention" of paper was a revolution in the information technology of his time.

The dry desert conditions at the caves of Dunhuang helped preserve many documents and works of art, including this tenth-century painting on paper of Prince Siddhartha, the future Buddha.

process of making paper mostly secret from the rest of the world, except Korea and Japan, until around the fifth century C.E. In 751 there was a war between an Arab army and the Tang Dynasty (618–907 C.E.) for control of part of the Silk Road. At one battle it is said that a number of Chinese papermakers were captured by the Arab army and taken back to Samarkand, in present-day Uzbekhistan. Certainly at around this time, paper began to be produced in the Arab world, and papermaking finally made its way to Europe in the twelfth century.

Making Paper

The basic process for making paper has changed very little from the earliest times. We have seen that the first Chinese paper was made from hemp. The fibers from the plant were soaked in water, washed, and beaten with wooden clubs or mallets until they became a pulp. A kind of sieve made of coarse cloth in a bamboo frame was then dipped into the watery pulp and lifted out. This drained the water from the pulp and helped form it into uniformly shaped sheets as it dried. However, the coarseness of the cloth in these sieves was probably one of the main reasons early paper was not suitable for writing on because the resulting surface was too uneven.

There were two further developments that revolutionized the use of paper, and Cai Lun was responsible for one of them at least. He experimented with using different fibers and materials as the basic ingredients. The second advance came with the development of a smooth material for the "sieve." Instead of using cloth, the ancient Chinese found that they could use thin strips of bamboo tied together to form a mat. Bamboo also had the strength to withstand being pressed very firmly to remove the water. This new method gave the paper a smoother texture, and made it easier to remove from the frame quickly and neatly so that the frame could be

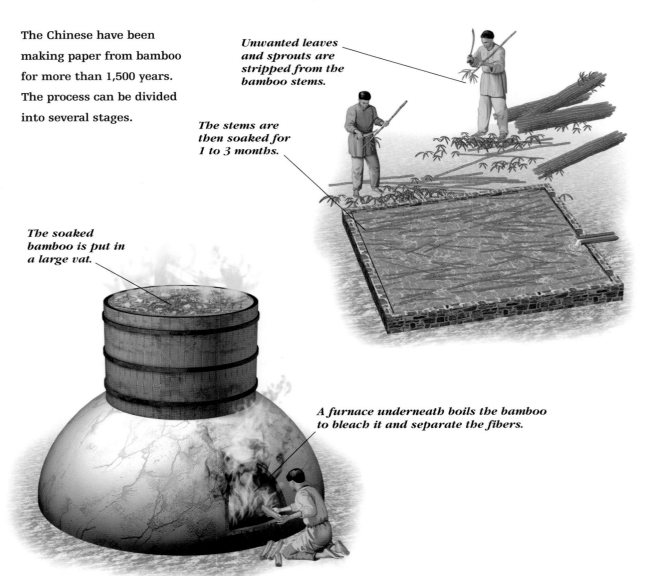

The Chinese have been making paper from bamboo for more than 1,500 years. The process can be divided into several stages.

Unwanted leaves and sprouts are stripped from the bamboo stems.

The stems are then soaked for 1 to 3 months.

The soaked bamboo is put in a large vat.

A furnace underneath boils the bamboo to bleach it and separate the fibers.

used again almost immediately. The ancient Chinese continued to improve this process, and to use new raw materials, such as bamboo and rice plants, to make different types of paper for different uses. The growth of Buddhism, with its many scriptures, gave a new impetus to papermaking in addition to the constant demand from imperial government, and was one inspiration that led to the invention of wood-block printing. Certainly the earliest known dated, complete printed book is a copy of a Buddhist sacred text, the *Diamond Sutra*, dating to 868 C.E.

Printing with movable type was said to have been invented by a man called Bi Sheng (990–1051 C.E.), who experimented with type made out of both pottery and wood. The Chinese language, however, was not well suited to this kind of printing, because individual letters are not used to form different words—each character needed its own separate block of type, meaning that several thousand might be needed for a single book. However, the

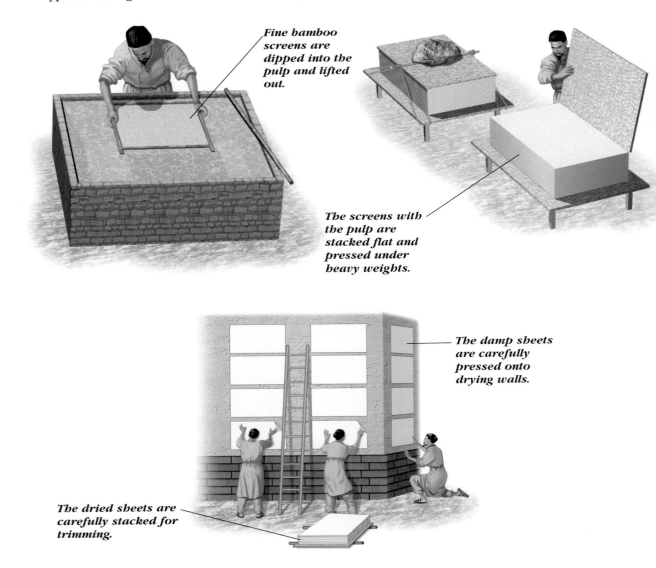

Fine bamboo screens are dipped into the pulp and lifted out.

The screens with the pulp are stacked flat and pressed under heavy weights.

The damp sheets are carefully pressed onto drying walls.

The dried sheets are carefully stacked for trimming.

The archaeologist Aurel Stein discovered this copy of the *Diamond Sutra* in a sealed cave at Dunhuang in 1907. It was made in 868 C.E. and is the earliest dated printed book in the world.

Uyghur people of Central Asia took on the idea of movable type and many books were printed in their language using this method starting in the 1200s. Movable metal type was first invented in Korea in around 1230.

Paper Money

Economists might argue that the greatest Chinese invention of all is that of paper money. It is difficult to say exactly when the idea started because paper money is mentioned in documents from various times starting in the Han Dynasty. Sometimes war or other emergencies made the

1600 B.C.E.	400 B.C.E.	200 B.C.E.		200 C.E.
Earliest writing on oracle bones	Earliest writing on bamboo strips	First Emperor Qin orders the use of a single script across China	Earliest paper	Earliest paper with writing on Cai Lun (d. 121 C.E.)

transportation of coins difficult or dangerous, and sometimes there was a shortage of copper, one of the metals that was normally used to make coins. Although silk was used as a currency, and also gold and silver, a standard form of money starting from the time of First Emperor Qin (259–210 B.C.E.) and onward was *banliang*, a round coin with a square hole in its center. The holes in the coins were used to string the coins together on cords or stack them on rods. However, transporting large quantities of heavy copper coins must have been troublesome, especially in a country of such huge dimensions as China, let alone the enormous distances over which trade was carried out along the Silk Road.

The Chinese called the first paper money "flying money," because it could be carried so easily across long distances, or, possibly because if you were not careful it could blow out of your hand. It was not the same as the bank notes we use today, but took the form of letters of credit exchanged by merchants promising payment in gold or coins in the future. This is the same principle on which modern banks and governments issue bank notes, but no one now bothers to go along and exchange them for actual gold or coins. The bank notes themselves take on the value of the money they represent.

The government under the Tang Dynasty (618–907 C.E.) was the first to see the possibilities of paper money, and began to use the merchants' system of letters of credit to move taxes around the country. It was not until the Song Dynasty (960–1279 C.E.), however, that the first actual paper money was issued officially by the government, in 1023 C.E. Unfortunately they did not fully understand the implications of this new idea, and within ten years all the banks that had issued the new paper money had run into trouble and had to close. The idea remained, however, and one hundred years later the government again began issuing paper money on a large scale, mainly to help pay for military campaigns. This was the time when paper money began to take on its own value. People no longer had the right to demand real cash in exchange for their notes. This also made it much more tempting to create fake paper money, and there now began a battle, which continues to this day, between the banks and governments printing paper money, and forgers and counterfeiters who try to make their own. Even in the twelfth century, Chinese banks began to use different colors in their banknotes, to make the designs more and more complicated, and even to use secret recipes for making the paper. Bank notes also started to be numbered. All these measures were to try to stop forgers making fake money, and the penalty for anyone caught doing so was death.

400 C.E.	600 C.E.	800 C.E.	1000 C.E.
	Smooth, fine paper produced from hemp and mulberry	Diamond Sutra: Earliest printed book	First paper money printed

Chinese emperors from the Song Dynasty onward tried issuing paper money, but none of them fully understood how it worked. This bank note from 1374 C.E. had a value of 1,000 bronze coins.

Spending Beyond Their Means

At the beginning, the system of paper money worked very well. However, this did not last. The Yuan emperors spent a great deal more money than they could afford to—especially on unsuccessful attempts to invade Japan and Vietnam. They also did not understand how to control such a large economy run on paper money. Inflation set in. Two new sets of notes were issued during the Yuan Dynasty (1279–1368 C.E.), each time reducing the value of the old notes five times. In the end, the notes were worth 25 times less than the gold or silver they originally represented, and people no longer trusted them. Although the next dynasty, the Ming (1368–1644 C.E.) also tried to introduce paper money, they were even less successful and at the end, their paper money was worth 300 times less than it was issued for. But even though paper money did not really work out for its inventors, the idea of it did spread to Europe and the West, where it took firm root and extended around the financial world.

Paper Factories

As the demand for paper grew, its production became more and more organized. Many of the early illustrations of the papermaking process seem to show that, much like silk production, it started as a peasant industry, with whole households and villages devoted to it. However, by the sixteenth century two provinces in the south of China, Fujian and Jiangxi (*Jee'ang-she*), had become the paper-manufacturing centers of China. At the end of the sixteenth century in Jiangxi, there were 60,000 workers running 600 mills and 30 factories making paper. In one year they could produce 50,000,000 sheets of paper using 30 billion bundles of rice straw.

Paper Facts and Figures

The Chinese did not use paper just for writing. Coarse hemp paper was used to wrap valuable objects. Pharmacists put their medicines into paper packages, and there is even a suggestion that paper handkerchiefs were in use in the first century B.C.E. It is certain that the Chinese were the inventors of toilet paper, which was being used by the sixth century C.E. We even have some impressive statistics for one year in the court of the early Ming Dynasty (1368–1644 C.E.): 720,000 sheets of straw paper measuring 2 feet by 3 feet (0.6 meters by 0.9 meters) were made for the court as a whole, and an extra 15,000 smaller, softer, perfumed sheets were made especially for members of the royal family. Apart from hats, paper-fabric made from the bark of the paper-mulberry tree was very practical because it was long-lasting, warm, and comfortable. It was even soft enough to make blankets. At the other extreme, the Chinese also found a way of making paper so hard that it could be used to make armor, which was said to be able to keep out not just arrows, but even bullets. There were countless other uses for paper in ancient China. When drinking tea for pleasure, rather than as a medicine, became popular in the Tang Dynasty (618–907 C.E.), people even had teabags and paper cups to drink from. The Chinese also invented wallpaper, paper umbrellas, and paper flowers.

Marco Polo Writes About Paper Money

The most famous account of the early use of paper money in China comes from the book written by the Venetian traveler Marco Polo about his voyages to and from the court of Kublai Khan (1215–1294 C.E.), the first emperor of the Yuan Dynasty (1279–1368 C.E.) and grandson of the famous Mongol leader Genghis Khan (c. 1162–1227 C.E.). The story of paper money under the Yuan Dynasty reflects what happened to the dynasty itself. Marco Polo thought paper money was almost like a kind of magic. He wrote:

The Emperor's Mint is also in the City of Cambaluc, and it is run in such a way that you might think he has discovered the secret of alchemy—and you would be right! There, by his orders, they take the bark of a certain tree—the mulberry tree, the leaves of which are also the food for silkworms and which grow in such great numbers that they fill whole districts. From between the outer bark of the tree and the actual wood of the tree they extract a fine white fiber or skin, which they make into something that resembles sheets of paper, except it is black. They then cut these sheets into pieces of different sizes.

He then goes on to describe how the money is made official:

These pieces of paper are issued officially with the same solemnity and authority as if they were gold or silver; there are officers whose duty it is to write their names and put their seals on each of these pieces of paper. When all the preliminary preparations are done, the Chief Officer appointed by the Khan uses his seal loaded with red ink to print the form of the seal on the paper—this makes the paper official currency. The penalty for anyone forging it is death.

Finally, and this is what impresses Marco most of all, he talks about how the system is used across the whole empire, and how Kublai Khan makes every merchant who comes into his territory swap their actual gold, silver, and jewels for this paper money.

He [the Emperor] *uses these pieces of paper, made as I have described above, to make all official payments on his account; he orders them to be used wherever his rule extends, throughout all his kingdoms, provinces, and territories. Nobody, however grand or important they consider themselves, dares to refuse them on pain of death …*

Moreover, any merchant arriving from India or elsewhere carrying gold, silver, precious stones or pearls is not allowed to sell them to anyone except the Emperor. He has appointed twelve experts, clever and experienced men of business, whose job it is to value the precious materials, and the Emperor then pays a generous price for them in those pieces of paper. The merchants are willing to accept the Emperor's offer firstly because they would not get such a good price anywhere else, and secondly because they are paid promptly. They can then use this paper to buy whatever they like throughout the Empire, and they find it very convenient, as the paper is many times lighter to carry around than gold or silver. Many of the merchants will make the journey several times in a year bringing goods of great value into the empire, and the Emperor buys it all with that paper. In this way he acquires a seemingly endless fortune, but the money he uses costs him nothing.

The Yuan Emperor Kublai Khan made every merchant who came to China exchange his goods for paper money. The merchants found this very convenient and it made the emperor very rich.

Chapter Four

Amazing Machines

A number of inventions from ancient China stand out as extraordinary. A machine for detecting earthquakes, and clocks that could chart the movements of the heavens, can only be described as truly astonishing. And yet, it is some of the discoveries that seem to us so commonplace which are the most important. The plow, the horse harness, and the wheelbarrow all changed the course of ancient Chinese, and world, history.

Zhang Heng was one of the greatest scientists in Chinese history. He was born in Nanyang in Henan province in 78 C.E. during the Han Dynasty (206 B.C.E.–220 C.E.). He was an artist, a poet, a writer, an inventor, a geographer, a mathematician, and an astronomer. In his youth he concentrated on studying literature and writing poetry. Some of his poems were preserved in a collection put together 400 years after his death, which has survived to the present day. Even as a poet he brought a sharp critical mind and accurate observation to his work. This has given us a lot of information about the Han capital of Chang'an. He even seems to have written some poems that were critical of the emperor—a daring thing to do.

At the age of 30, Zhang turned from literature to science. He began to study mathematics and astronomy, and was soon publishing scholarly works on the subjects. He came to the notice of the imperial government

This is a model of an armillary sphere, or model of the heavens, built for the Yuan Emperor Kublai Khan in 1279 by his chief astronomer Guo Shoujing.

51

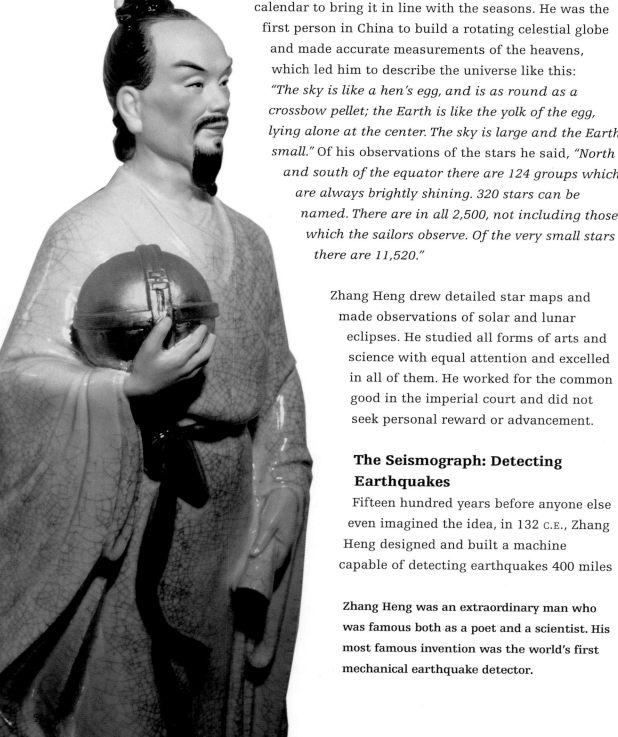

and was appointed to a series of official posts, ending up as Chief Astronomer to the court of Emperor An. He is most famous for inventing the first seismograph, a machine for detecting earthquakes. He developed grids and scales to make maps more accurate. He calculated one of the earliest practical approximations of the value of *pi*, the ratio of a circle's circumference to its diameter. He corrected the calendar to bring it in line with the seasons. He was the first person in China to build a rotating celestial globe and made accurate measurements of the heavens, which led him to describe the universe like this: *"The sky is like a hen's egg, and is as round as a crossbow pellet; the Earth is like the yolk of the egg, lying alone at the center. The sky is large and the Earth small."* Of his observations of the stars he said, *"North and south of the equator there are 124 groups which are always brightly shining. 320 stars can be named. There are in all 2,500, not including those which the sailors observe. Of the very small stars there are 11,520."*

Zhang Heng drew detailed star maps and made observations of solar and lunar eclipses. He studied all forms of arts and science with equal attention and excelled in all of them. He worked for the common good in the imperial court and did not seek personal reward or advancement.

The Seismograph: Detecting Earthquakes

Fifteen hundred years before anyone else even imagined the idea, in 132 C.E., Zhang Heng designed and built a machine capable of detecting earthquakes 400 miles

Zhang Heng was an extraordinary man who was famous both as a poet and a scientist. His most famous invention was the world's first mechanical earthquake detector.

(644 kilometers) away. This was not just an example of a clever scientist showing off—the invention was of great practical use. China is a country of earthquakes—the earliest recorded one took place in 1177 B.C.E. and through history the country has seen some of the most destructive earthquakes in the world. In 1556 three provinces were struck by an earthquake that is reported to have killed 800,000 people.

Zhang Heng only built one seismograph, which did not survive the centuries. Scientists have made reconstructions of it based on descriptions in books, but no one knows exactly how it actually worked.

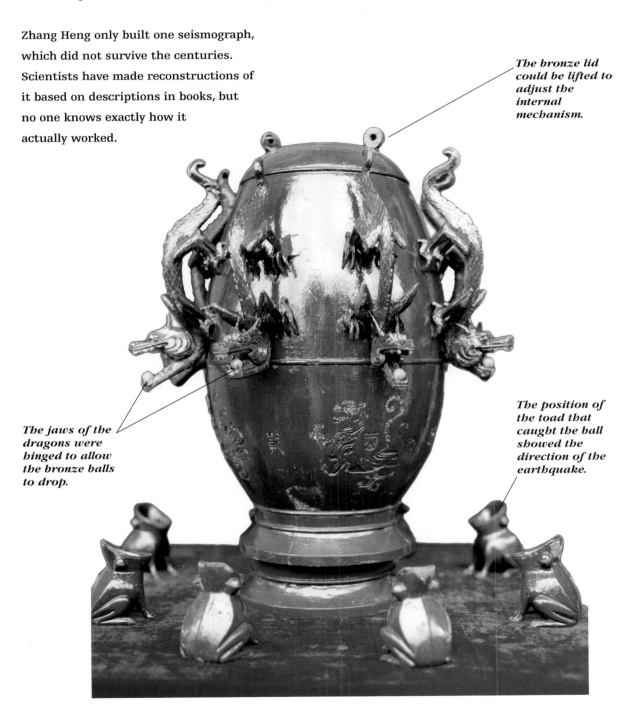

The bronze lid could be lifted to adjust the internal mechanism.

The jaws of the dragons were hinged to allow the bronze balls to drop.

The position of the toad that caught the ball showed the direction of the earthquake.

Zhang Heng's seismograph was called the *houfeng didong yi* (instrument for measuring the seasonal winds and the movements of the earth). It was not able to predict earthquakes, but it was able to tell the imperial court in which direction the disaster had happened. This was very important because it gave the court warning of all the problems that earthquakes brought with them, including food shortages, transportation problems, and even the possibility of rebellion. They then knew at least that the earthquake had happened and in which direction to send for more news.

Dragons and Toads

So, what did Zhang's instrument look like and how did it work? The principle was very simple, but the imagination and engineering involved were remarkable for the time. The whole thing was made of bronze. The main body was a huge jar, 6 feet (1.82 meters) across in the body with a short, narrow neck, and beautifully decorated with traditional designs of mountains, birds, and animals. Regularly spaced around the outside of the jar were eight bronze dragons or dragons' heads, each holding a bronze ball in its mouth. Directly underneath each dragon, on the base of the instrument, were placed eight bronze models of toads with great gaping mouths.

No one knows precisely how the machinery inside the jar was constructed, because the device itself disappeared centuries ago, and there are no pictures, only descriptions. Various modern scholars have made reconstructions of Zhang's instrument to demonstrate their theories on

The mechanism of Zhang Heng's seismograph was so sensitive, we know that it once detected an earthquake 400 miles (644 km) away from the imperial court.

how it worked. It seems most likely that inside was something like the arm of a metronome or upside-down pendulum that would sway in the direction from which any slight tremor came. As it swayed it would push a rod or activate a catch that allowed the bronze ball to fall from the mouth of the dragon into the waiting toad's mouth. The *History of the Later Han* describes it like this:

Now although the mechanism of one dragon was released, the seven [other] *heads did not move, and by following the direction* [of the dragon which had been set in motion], *one knew (the direction) from which the earthquake had come.*

It was one thing, of course, for Zhang Heng to tell people what he believed his machine could do, but another to convince them that it worked. However, as the *History of the Later Han* tells us:

On one occasion one of the dragons let fall a ball from its mouth though no perceptible shock could be felt. All the scholars at the capital were astonished at this strange effect occurring without any evidence (of an earthquake to cause it). But several days later a messenger arrived bringing news of an earthquake in Long-Xi (400 miles [644 kilometers] away to the northwest). *Upon this everyone admitted the mysterious power of the instrument. Thenceforward it became the duty of the officials of the Bureau of Astronomy and Calendar to record the directions from which earthquakes came.*

Water Clocks

The Chinese sometimes claim that they invented the water clock independently of other civilizations who also used this device in ancient times. However, it is perhaps even more exciting to think that even in the very earliest times, ideas and knowledge were traveling vast distances across the continents. Both the Babylonians and the ancient Egyptians knew about simple water clocks as early as 1600 B.C.E., and most scholars now believe that this is where the Chinese got the idea. Although they were used partly for simply telling the time, water clocks, particularly in China, were very important for astrology and astronomy.

The simplest kind of water clock is called an outflow clock. Here, water drips out through a hole in the bottom of a container, and the falling level of the water in the container measures the passing of time. The earliest mention of such a device in China is a book called the *Zhou Li*, which was probably written in the fourth century B.C.E. The Chinese seem to have advanced rapidly from the simple outflow clock to the inflow system. At its basic level the inflow clock is very similar, the only difference is that the water flows into a container and it is the rising level in this container that is measured.

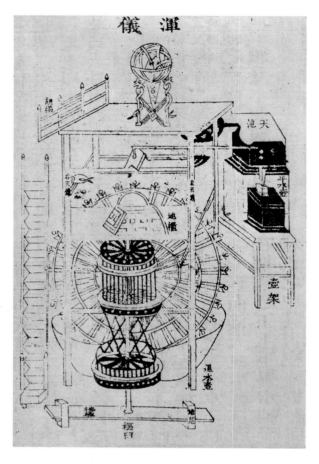

This is a later drawing of the workings of one of the first water-driven astronomical clocks. It shows the double water-tank invented by Zhang Heng, and the large multi-spoked waterwheel.

Historians believe that it was Zhang Heng who first devised an improved method of regulating water clocks. The main problem was that the rate of flow of water changes in a simple water clock as the water level, and therefore pressure, gets lower. Zhang realized that if you put at least one extra tank in the middle of the system it is much easier to keep the water flow at the end constant. All manner of other factors could also affect the flow of the water, especially air temperature and humidity, so telling the time accurately by this method was never completely reliable. In fact, the Chinese became more interested in using water clocks as a source of power for more complicated astronomical instruments. A Buddhist monk named Yixing (*ee-shing*) built the first of these complex instruments in 725 C.E. It was called the "Water-driven Spherical Bird's-Eye-View Map of the Heavens." This was a bronze sphere powered by a water-turned wheel regulated so that it made one complete turn in 24 hours. From this, two outer rings were powered, representing the sun and the moon. With this machine it was said to be possible to make exact calculations of the times of sunrise and sunset, and also the full and new moons. In 976 C.E., a man called Zhang Sixun (*Jang-Suh-shoo'un*) built an even more ambitious clock, which he powered with flowing mercury to avoid the problem of the clock stopping when the water froze. The clock was enclosed in a wooden tower that was three stories—30 feet (9 meters)—high. It functioned as a clock, ringing the quarter hours and marking the traditional two-hour divisions of the Chinese day. There was also a celestial globe, which showed the movements of the sun, the moon, and five planets.

Another of China's famous scholars, Su Song (1020–1101 C.E.), built the greatest Chinese clock of all during the Song Dynasty (960–1127 C.E.). Su Song was famous in many different fields of study and science including zoology, botany, chemistry, and mapmaking, as well as being a politician and a diplomat. He is best remembered, however, for the huge astronomical clock tower he built in the northern Chinese city of Kaifeng. We know a great deal about this clock,

Gunpowder and Guns

Gunpowder—called *huo yao* (fire chemical) in Chinese—is a mixture of saltpeter (potassium nitrate), sulfur, and charcoal. Alchemists in ancient China experimented with these ingredients in their search for the secret of eternal life. A book called *Cantong Qi* or The Kinship of Three written by Wei Boyang in 142 C.E. is the first to record a recipe for something that resembles gunpowder. There were stern warnings about using this particular combination of ingredients because they were known to cause dangerous and unpredictable fires. Nevertheless people continued to experiment, and the first controlled use of a form of gunpowder seems to have been in making louder and better firecrackers. The first firecrackers, used at ceremonies and festivals to frighten off evil spirits, were probably just sections of green bamboo thrown onto a fire. The air and moisture in the hollow bamboo caused them to explode. At some stage, people realized that packing the bamboo with *huo yao* would make a bigger and better bang, and so fireworks were born.

This early form of gunpowder continued to be used for making fireworks, but it was probably not until the 900s C.E. that its use in warfare began to be explored. At first it was used to make fuses, or attached to arrows in bundles that would start fires where they landed. Experiments with different proportions of saltpeter in the formula led ancient Chinese scientists to discover the true explosive potential of *huo yao*. In the first half of the eleventh century, "thunderclap bombs" were being hurled into besieged cities by catapult, made from gunpowder packed into bamboo or paper casings. These soon developed into smaller hand-held grenades. By the twelfth century, iron casings were developed for the bombs, which meant that they could be made so powerful that blasts could be heard more than 10 miles (16 km) away. Floating bombs that could drift down a river to sink enemy boats are known from the fourteenth century, two hundred years earlier than the first use of a sea-mine in Europe.

The first gun to be invented in China, at the beginning of the tenth century, was more of a flame-thrower than a true gun, with a barrel made from bamboo. Soon these were replaced by metal barrels. A metal-barreled handgun dating from 1288 excavated in Heilongjiang (*Hey-long-jee'ang*) province included a smooth bore, a touch-hole for lighting the powder, and a reinforced explosion chamber. It is likely that around this time the secrets of gunpowder and gun-making were transported from China to the Middle East and Europe.

This is a military incendiary rocket, called the magic flying burning crow, invented in the Ming Dynasty. It could fly over 1,150 feet (350 meters) and was designed to set fire to the enemy's stores and provisions.

A Secret Weapon: The Wheelbarrow

Like the plow, it is easy to take some of the simplest inventions for granted, and hard even to think of them as inventions. One example of this is the wheelbarrow. The wheelbarrow seems such a simple idea, but there is no concrete evidence of its existence in the west until the twelfth or thirteenth century C.E. The Chinese invention of this deceptively basic form of transportation is attributed to a (possibly mythical) Daoist priest called Ko Yu who is rather mysteriously said to have built a wooden goat and ridden away on it. It is not clear when Ko Yu lived, if he in fact existed, but the first pictures of wheelbarrows are seen in Han Dynasty tombs of the second century C.E.

When talking about Chinese wheelbarrows, we must try to forget our own Western ideas about them in two major ways. From the earliest times, Chinese wheelbarrows were much better balanced even than modern Western ones. The wheel was near the center of the cart, which made the whole thing much lighter to push, or to pull, because some were designed with the handles facing forward. The second difference is in their use. Wheelbarrows are normally thought of as commonplace tools used by laborers and farmers, but in China they were used as a piece of top-secret military equipment with several different functions. Some were designed to carry supplies across rugged mountain terrain, and others were troop transports for carrying soldiers up to battle. Some were even used in battalions as a flexible and instantly adjustable defensive wall against cavalry attack. Later on, of course, the wheelbarrow was used for ordinary, everyday tasks, but at one time it was China's secret weapon.

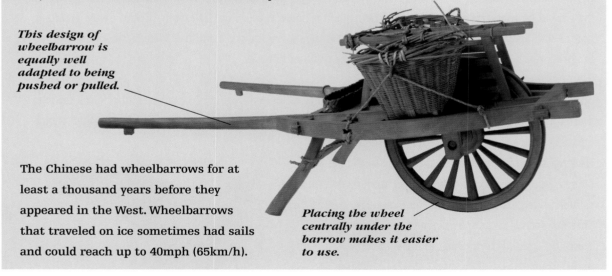

This design of wheelbarrow is equally well adapted to being pushed or pulled.

The Chinese had wheelbarrows for at least a thousand years before they appeared in the West. Wheelbarrows that traveled on ice sometimes had sails and could reach up to 40mph (65km/h).

Placing the wheel centrally under the barrow makes it easier to use.

200 B.C.E.		300 C.E.
Qin Dynasty 221–206 B.C.E.	Han Dynasty 206 B.C.E.–220 C.E.	**Period of Disunity**
First Emperor Qin 259–210 B.C.E.	**Du Shi** d. 38 C.E. **Zhang Heng** 78–139 C.E.	

Experts used the instructions in Su Song's own book to make this scale-model of his giant astronomical clock. Although powered by water, it had a complex system of gears that made it very accurate.

This bronze sphere showed the movements of the planets and stars.

The huge water-wheel traveled forward by one scoop every 15 minutes.

Su Song's mechanism was the model for future clocks in China and eventually the West.

The whole clock stood more than 30 feet (9 meters) high.

completed in 1094 C.E.—although it no longer survives—because a book he wrote about building it still exists, complete with illustrations. Su's clock was powered by a giant waterwheel, and the mechanism was contained in a wooden tower at least 30 feet (9 meters) high, like Zhang Sixun's clock. On top of Su's tower was a huge bronze sphere representing the heavens and the position of the stars. This was balanced, inside the tower, by another globe representing the earth, which moved in perfect synchronization with the one above. Miniature

		800 C.E.		1200 C.E.	
	Sui Dynasty 589–618 C.E.	**Tang Dynasty 618–907 C.E.**		**Song Dynasty 960–1279 C.E.**	
				Su Song 1020–1101 C.E.	

human models appeared, rang bells telling the hours of the day, and then disappeared. Su combined his mathematical genius with his engineering skills to make a chain drive for the clock, which powered some very precise gears, so the accuracy of this clock was greater than anything that had been achieved before.

Su Song's clock ran for thirty-four years, twenty-five years after its inventor's death, until, at the fall of the Song Dynasty, the Mongols captured it. They moved it to their new capital in Beijing, but some stories say they were not able to reassemble it properly and it never worked consistently again. Nevertheless, it paved the way for the future development of mechanical clocks in China, and was almost certainly the original source of knowledge for clockmakers in the West.

Making Iron: Blast Furnaces, Swords, and Plows

A blast furnace is a special kind of very hot "oven" used to get a metal—usually iron—from the raw ore in which it is mined. Blast furnaces existed in China almost 2,000 years before the process was discovered in Europe. Since late Neolithic times (7000–2000 B.C.E.), the Chinese had been skilled at making furnaces that could generate very high temperatures. Originally these were used as kilns for firing pottery and then as furnaces for melting bronze. A blast furnace is so-called because air is "blasted" into the bottom of the furnace while the raw material is fed in at the top. This process is known as smelting. As the smelting process takes place, molten metal and waste solids come out at the bottom of the furnace, and gases escape from the top.

The earliest blast furnaces almost certainly developed from bronze-casting technology, and by the fifth century B.C.E., good-quality cast-iron farm tools and weapons were being produced. However, the earliest blast furnaces for which there is direct evidence date from the first century B.C.E. during the early Han Dynasty, and it was at this time that the technology improved dramatically too. A government official called Du Shi saw the possibility of combining two existing technologies to make blast furnaces more efficient. It is recorded:

In the seventh year of the Jian Wu reign period [31 C.E.] Du Shi was posted to be Prefect of Nanyang. He was a generous man and his policies were peaceful; he destroyed evildoers and established the dignity [of his office]. Good at planning, he loved the common people and wished to save their labor. He invented a water-powered machine for casting [iron] agricultural implements. Those who smelted and cast already had the push-bellows to blow their charcoal fires, and now they were instructed to use the rushing of the water to operate it…. Thus the people got great benefit for little labor. They found the "water [-powered] bellows" convenient and adopted it widely.

In other words, Du Shi devised a way of powering bellows with a waterwheel, which meant that the air could be pumped into the furnace much more powerfully and more regularly. From this time on, the Chinese became masters of iron technology.

There is evidence, however, that even from sometime before these developments took place, the Chinese had been producing a type of steel. The founder of the Han Dynasty (206 B.C.E.–220 C.E.), Liu Bang (256–195 B.C.E.), is said to have had a magnificent steel sword. This is something that could not have been created in Europe until at least the sixteenth century, almost 2,000 years later.

The Chinese invented the blast furnace for smelting iron very early in their history. It was very important for the mass production of weapons and agricultural tools.

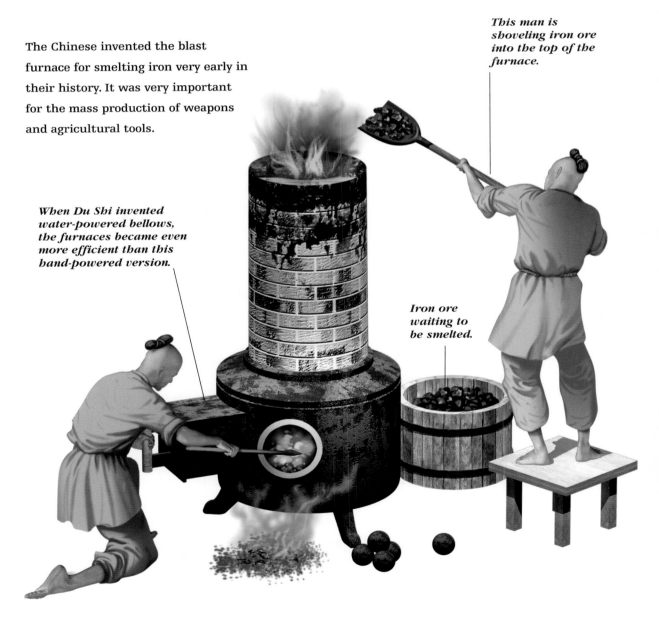

This man is shoveling iron ore into the top of the furnace.

When Du Shi invented water-powered bellows, the furnaces became even more efficient than this hand-powered version.

Iron ore waiting to be smelted.

A craftsman called Ma San made this bronze blunderbuss in 1332. It is the earliest known gun of its type. It fired a stone bullet loaded through the muzzle.

Iron had two principal uses in early China, as weapons and as farm tools. Both were of equal importance. By the time of First Emperor Qin (259–210 B.C.E.) most of the kingdoms of China were using iron as the main metal for weapons. Strangely, the exception to this was First Emperor Qin himself, who continued to use bronze for his armies. Iron, however, was vital to the First Emperor for nonmilitary purposes, and he developed a highly organized iron industry, producing tools for his massive palace and road- and wall-building projects.

Outside the lofty worlds of emperors and scientists, China has always been a country that relied on farming, and its agricultural implements have always been advanced. A highly efficient form of plow, not known in the West for many centuries, was in use in China starting in the fourth century B.C.E. This design was made even more efficient by the development of a kind of iron for the plowshare that did not shatter easily. During the Han Dynasty a network of iron foundries was established throughout the country to mass-produce these high-quality farm implements. This meant they were available to every farmer, no matter how poor, which helped ensure the production of enough food to supply such a vast country. In fact, it may be said that the square-framed iron-bladed plow was more important than any other invention in ensuring China's prosperity through the ages.

Efficient Pulling Power: Inventing the Harness

It seems almost unbelievable that no other civilization in ancient times—and there were many that considered themselves expert with horses—managed to invent an efficient harness. For centuries riders relied on an arrangement called the throat-and-girth harness, which meant the poor horse had constant pressure on its neck and windpipe. The Chinese started this way too but, sometime around the fourth century B.C.E., a new arrangement was devised with a strap across the chest of the horse rather than its neck. This is known as the trace, or breast-strap, harness and it doubled the load a horse was comfortably able to pull. Two hundred years later, the Chinese had come up with an even better harness, which is still used all around the world today. This is the collar harness, in which a padded collar is placed around the chest of the horse. It provides a raised attachment point for the yoke of the cart to be pulled and allows the breastbone rather than the neck to take the strain. It is possible that the inspiration for this collar came from those used on camels, which the Chinese were becoming more familiar with as trading on the Silk Road began.

The collar harness has been shown to be three times more efficient than the original throat-and-girth harness. In China the collar harness was in general use by the first century B.C.E., but the trace harness didn't reach Europe until the sixth century C.E., and the collar harness was unknown there until the tenth century C.E. So just as the advanced development of the plow maximized China's food production from the earliest times, so their horse harness speeded its distribution—two huge factors in China's continuity and success as a world civilization.

China developed an efficient horse harness much more quickly than the West. The collar harness made it easy for horses to pull very heavy loads.

The high attachment point imitated the hump on an ox.

With this harness a horse could pull anything from a farm cart to an imperial chariot.

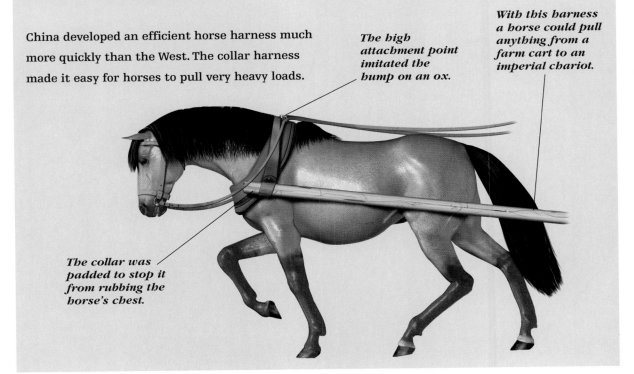

The collar was padded to stop it from rubbing the horse's chest.

Chapter Five

Medicine and Feng Shui

Hundreds of years before the beginnings of modern Western medicine, the ancient Chinese developed and refined a complex system for understanding the human body, how it works, and its place in nature. Medical science took great strides in China during the Han Dynasty (206 B.C.E.–220 C.E.), and benefited from advances and ideas that traveled along the Silk Road from India and even Greece. Although today we see acupuncture and herbal medicine as the two main strands of Chinese medicine, in ancient times these different treatments were closely linked.

Only six years into the Tang Dynasty, in 624 C.E., the emperor decreed the establishment of the *Taiyiju* (Imperial Medical Bureau). The Taiyiju was responsible for overseeing education in many fields of medicine and continued to run throughout the Tang Dynasty. In the Song Dynasty that followed (960–1127 C.E.), a man called Wang Anshi brought about some very important reforms of the government system in all fields. Among these were changes in both the administration and the teaching of medicine, and the Imperial Medical College was set up in the Song capital at Kaifeng. The College was at the forefront of advancing medical technology.

Pins and Needles: Acupuncture

The mythological Huang Di, whose name means Yellow Emperor, was, according to legend, the father of acupuncture. He is also said to be the author of the first medical text, the *Yellow Emperor's Classic of Internal Medicine*, which he is

According to legend, Shen Nong, the Divine Farmer, gave the Chinese people the gift of herbal medicine.

A Demanding Course

During the Song Dynasty (960–1279 C.E.), out of the entire, vast country, only three hundred students were admitted to the Imperial Medical College. They had to take an entrance examination, and from those results the students were divided into three grades with only forty in the top grade. The students had to study nine different areas of medicine under the top doctors and teachers in the empire, who included acupuncturists, pediatricians, gynecologists, ophthalmologists, and dentists, and there was a special department for the study of war wounds.

Students did not just study textbooks. During their time in the college they also acted as doctors for the other government departments and for the army. In this way they gained experience in treating many different patients and conditions. On top of their exams they also had to keep very detailed records of all the people they treated and any student who did not cure at least half of his patients was expelled from the college. The students took tests every month with a full examination at the end of the year. Every two years they had a chance to move up a grade. At the top grade, before graduating, students were marked not just on their medical knowledge but also on whether they had behaved well over the previous years.

supposed to have written around 5,000 years ago. In fact, it was compiled sometime between 305 and 204 B.C.E. It contains the first written references to acupuncture, which is called *zhen bian* in Chinese. Acupuncture is a system of medicine that uses needles to take away pain and cure illnesses.

Acupuncture is closely related to the Chinese philosophy of Daoism, which believes that there is a universal energy in nature that must be kept in balance. This energy is called *qi* (*chee*) and the balance is between *yin* (female, dark) and *yang*, (male, light). In acupuncture it is believed that *qi* flows throughout our bodies but can sometimes become blocked. Different things can disturb the flow of *qi*, whether they are physical, psychological, or emotional. For example, acupuncturists believe that anger, stress, fear, grief, poor nutrition, poison, infection, or injuries can all upset the balance of *yin* and *yang* and block the flow of *qi*. Acupuncturists aim to restore the balance and flow of *qi* by inserting fine needles into the

Nowadays the **yin** and **yang** symbol is recognized all over the world. The combination of the dark **yin** and light **yang** in the symbol represents the ideal balance of natural energy in the body.

Practicing Putting in Needles

In 1026 C.E. a famous doctor, Wang Weiyi, designed and commissioned two bronze figures on which were engraved all the acupuncture points and meridians. When it was time for student examinations, the hollow bodies of these figures were filled with water and the markings were covered with wax. The students had to locate given acupuncture points, and if they inserted their needles in the right place, water flowed out.

It took many years of study to become skilled in acupuncture. Models such as this copper man, made in the Qing Dynasty, helped doctors learn where to place their needles.

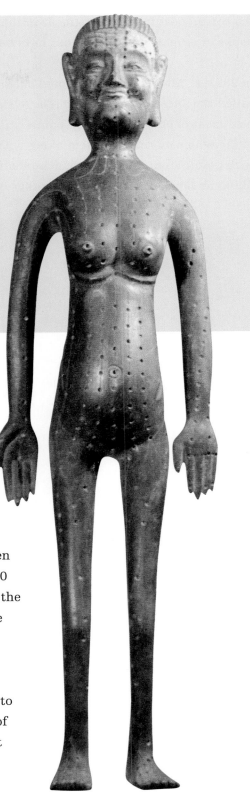

skin at different points along certain energy channels, called meridians. There are twelve principal meridians that link the organs of the body. Sticks of an herb called moxa are sometimes burned to apply heat during treatment. This is known as moxibustion.

The origins of acupuncture are not clear. Archaeologists have identified sharpened rocks and stones as being medical instruments. Needles have been found that date from the early Bronze Age (around 1500 B.C.E.), and one of the earliest Chinese characters from the same period has been shown to mean "stones that cure disease." The *Yellow Emperor's Classic of Internal Medicine* contains the first written description of the principles of acupuncture. It describes the meridians, acupuncture points, how to diagnose illness, and how to apply the needles. It also mentions moxibustion. One of the silk paintings from the Early Han Dynasty tomb at Mawangdui shows a diagram of the meridians on the human body but does not mark the acupuncture points. Nonetheless it is known that acupuncture was the commonest form of treatment in the Han Dynasty (206 B.C.E.–220 C.E.) and the names and books of several famous doctors have been identified.

In 282 C.E., Mi Huangfu completed one of the most important books in acupuncture. It was called the *Zhen Jiu Jia Yi Jing* (*The Systematic Classic of Acupuncture and Moxibustion*). It lists most of the acupuncture points still used today, and it gives a point-by-point description of the whole meridian system along with a detailed description of how to use the needle at each point. From this time on, acupuncture developed very rapidly and even spread outside China to Japan and Korea. Many other doctors contributed to the subject. Even the Mongols

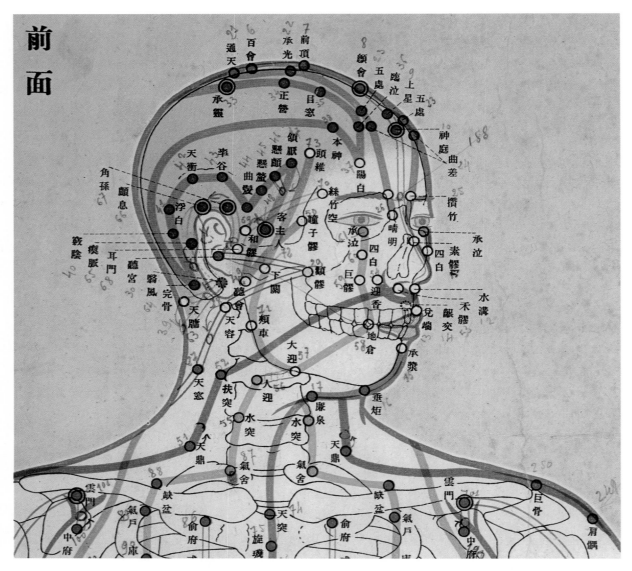

This illustration, showing acupuncture points on the head and neck, is from a modern edition of the first medical textbook on acupuncture, said to have been written by the mythical emperor Huang Di.

who invaded China under Kublai Khan (1215–1294 C.E.) encouraged the development of acupuncture.

Herbal Medicine

Along with acupuncture, herbal medicine is the other main branch of ancient Chinese medicine, and their histories are linked. Herbal medicine also has a mythical origin. According to ancient Chinese legend, Shen Nong, a legendary figure whose name means divine farmer, tasted all the herbs himself to try them out. Shen Nong is also supposed to have written a book, *The Divine Farmer's Herb-Root Classic,* which historians now know was actually put together in the Han Dynasty.

The legend of Shen Nong helps us understand several basic elements of Chinese herbal medicine. It also tells the story of how he is said to have discovered tea. While out gathering herbs one day, Shen Nong fell asleep under a certain type of bush. As he slept, some leaves from this bush fell into a cauldron of boiling water that he had prepared to

Doctors used hundreds of different plants to make medicines. Ones that looked similar might have different properties, so it was important to have accurate pictures and descriptions.

experiment with brewing the herbs he had gathered. When he woke up, he tasted the water and found that it was good to drink; his divine powers also showed him that this new drink was a powerful medicine that could cure the effects of seventy different types of poison. In fact for many centuries, tea in China was used only as a medicine. The young shoots were also eaten as a vegetable. It was only around 600 C.E. that it began to be enjoyed as a refreshing and social drink in the way it is today.

Unappetizing Ingredients

Some highly unusual herbs and other substances were used in ancient China, such as silkworm, bamboo shavings, turtle shell, hedgehog skin, ivy tree bark, toad skin, earthworm, "dragon bones," Mongolian Snakegourd Root, centipede, and scorpion. You might feel you would have to be very, very unwell in order to be convinced to take your medicine.

How Many Herbs?

Herbal medicine is also described in the *Yellow Emperor's Classic of Internal Medicine,* in which twenty-eight herbs and other substances and twelve prescriptions are mentioned. This is a tiny number when you consider how herbal medicine then developed. Looking at the number of herbs mentioned in Chinese medical books published over the centuries, there are 844 different herbs mentioned in 659 C.E., 1,558 in 1108 C.E., and 1,892 in 1596 C.E. The number is still growing. In one important book written in 500 C.E. herbs are classified in categories, such as "Superior Herbs nourish life," "Middle Herbs correct the constitution," and "Inferior Herbs drive out disease." This shows the most important aim of the ancient Chinese was to ensure things did not start to go wrong in the first place, so that curing an illness was only a last resort.

Ginseng root is one of the best known and most powerful traditional Chinese medicines. The stem, leaf, flower, and fruit of ginseng can also be used in treatments.

Preparing and Dispensing Medicine

The most common method of preparing traditional herbal medicines was by brewing them in hot or boiling water and then drinking the mixture. Some remedies might be made up of a single herb, but many of them involved complicated recipes including many different ingredients, each of which had to be very carefully measured in exact proportions. Some of these ingredients were commonly available and could be cultivated, but many of them, especially the most powerful ones, grew only in wild and remote places. The wise man going out to search for medicinal plants and mushrooms is a popular subject in Chinese poetry and painting.

Not all medicines were taken in the form of a mixture. In the early years of the twentieth century a great store of manuscripts was discovered at Dunhuang, in western China. One of these, dating from the eighth century C.E., reveals a remarkable parallel between ancient Chinese medicine and modern Western medicine. It describes a treatment for heart pain in which a fine powder of saltpeter (potassium nitrate) is placed under the tongue of the patient to mix with the saliva, and then swallowed. Modern Western doctors treat angina (heart pain) in a very similar way today, and the medicine is even delivered in exactly the same way.

Traditional herbal medicines may contain many different ingredients. In this picture a pharmacist is using scales to measure the exact amounts to make up a prescription from the jars on the shelves.

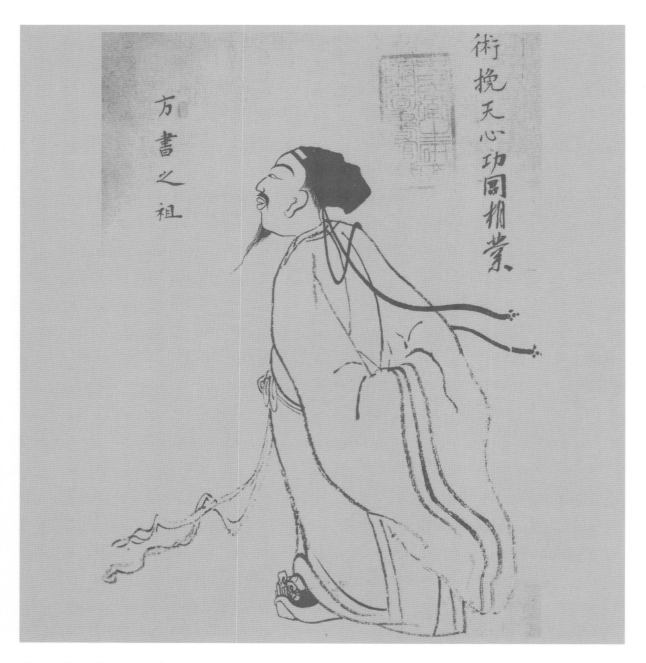

方書之祖

術挽天心功同相業

Zhang Zhongjing was a famous Han Dynasty doctor. He lived between about 150 and 219 C.E. and was an expert in the treatment of the epidemic diseases that caused millions of deaths in ancient China.

200 B.C.E.			300 C.E.
	Qin Dynasty 221–206 B.C.E.	**Han Dynasty 206 B.C.E.–220 C.E.**	**Period of Disunity**
305–204 B.C.E. *Yellow Emperor's Classic of Internal Medicine* **is compiled**		**100s C.E.** **Hua Tuo develops anesthesia and Zhang Zhongjing makes advances in herbal medicine**	**282 C.E.** **Mi Huangfu compiles** *Systematic Classic of Acupuncture and Moxibustion*

Three Famous Doctors

Throughout the history of Chinese medicine there have been doctors whose names have survived down to this day because of their great skill. Some even gained the status of "immortals" and are revered within the Daoist religion.

Hua Tuo (*Hwa-tor*) lived in the second century C.E. and is recorded as being the first doctor to use anesthesia to perform surgery. He used a potion made from hemp along with other herbs and wine. He treated many of the most famous generals of the late Han Dynasty, including the most famous, Cao Cao. He became Cao Cao's exclusive physician—a position that was to cost him his life. Hua Tuo diagnosed Cao Cao with a brain tumor and told him that he would need an operation to open up his skull and remove the growth. Cao Cao could not believe this and decided Hua Tuo was trying to assassinate him, and ordered his execution. Later, Cao's son fell ill and died and Cao cried out in regret that in executing Hua Tuo, his best physician, he had killed his own son.

Zhang Zhongjing (*Jang-jong-jing*) lived at the same time as Hua Tuo in the late Han Dynasty. He is revered as the most famous herbalist of all the ancient doctors. He compiled a book called *A Discussion of Diseases Caused by Cold*, which became the foundation for the future development of Chinese herbal medicine. It contains a hundred prescriptions, some of which are still in use today. He was inspired to write this book after China suffered a great plague that was said to have infected two-thirds of the population. Zhang Zhongjing was determined to find a cure and to stop such an epidemic from occurring again. Two modern treatments that Zhang is credited with pioneering are artificial respiration and fluid replacement.

Tao Hongjing (*Tow-hong-jing*) lived between 452 and 536 C.E. He spent his life studying the remedies in Shen Nong's *Divine Farmer's Herb-Root Classic*, re-editing it and adding 365 new herbs. From this he also wrote his own

Hua Tuo also developed a series of exercises for good health based on the movements of the tiger, deer, bear, ape, and crane.

			800 C.E.		1200 C.E.
	Sui Dynasty 589–618 C.E.	**Tang Dynasty 618–907 C.E.**			**Song Dynasty 960–1279 C.E.**
452–536 C.E. Tao Hongjing re-edits *The Divine Farmer's Herb-Root Classic*		**624 C.E.** Imperial Medical Bureau established			

book, which was the most important influence on the development of medicine during the Tang Dynasty.

A very simple story is told about Tao that reveals his interest in establishing scientific principles for medical treatment. At the time, there was a tale going around that birds grew out of worms. Tao did not believe this could be true, but instead of simply dismissing it, he settled down to make long and careful observations.

He concluded that worms were brought into the nests by parent birds. However, although they did indeed breed there, what they produced were more worms that served as food for the baby birds. The lesson that Tao learned from this and passed on to future generations of doctors was that one should not necessarily trust what others tell you, nor jump to conclusions, but should only proceed on the basis of careful observation.

Feng Shui: Living in Harmony

The Chinese words *feng* and *shui* literally mean wind and water, but together they have a different meaning. *Feng Shui* (*Fung-shoo'eh*) is a term that describes practices that have survived and evolved from the times of very ancient China right up to the present day. In the West many people are familiar with the simple idea that *Feng Shui* is about choosing the right house in the right place and arranging your rooms and their furniture in a way that will bring you good luck by helping positive energy to flow. In ancient times, however, the concept was used on a much grander and more important scale. *Feng Shui* was used to decide how cities should be laid out and where buildings, palaces, and tombs should be located.

Principles and Symbols

Feng Shui is closely connected with the idea, central to Chinese medicine, that *qi* (energy) must flow and that yin and yang should be in balance. *Feng Shui* is the means used to achieve this positive effect in the environment. The practice of *Feng Shui* evolved over thousands of years, and is linked to the study of the *Yijing*, or Classic of Changes. This ancient text is an interpretation of a set of symbols called trigrams, combinations of broken and unbroken lines which were used to foretell the future and in deciding which actions to take. Masters of *Feng Shui* used elements of astrology, combined with a knowledge of the *Yijing*, the Chinese landscape, and an understanding of human nature, to determine how all these factors could affect the future.

One of the most important symbols used in *Feng Shui* is the *bagua,* an eight-sided shape in which eight trigrams are aligned with the eight main points of the compass. These trigrams, along with other meanings associated with the compass points, can be interpreted in many complex ways and are the basic tool for working out the *Feng Shui* of places and buildings.

Feng Shui also uses the concept of the Five Elements in traditional Chinese belief: Earth, Metal, Wood, Fire, and Water. Each has its own properties and relationship with the others, for example Water puts out Fire, and Wood can be burned to make Fire. Balance between the Five Elements is very important.

The following example shows how modern concepts of *Feng Shui*, which still have their roots in ancient practice, can be used to determine the actions to take in everyday life. In traditional Chinese numerology, everyone is born on a date which relates to one of the Five Elements. Someone born in a Fire year should avoid having ponds or aquariums in their home, because Water extinguishes Fire. On the other hand, having lots of green plants, which symbolize Wood, would be a benefit to them. Fire also represents the south, so placing their bed in the southern part of their house would bring good fortune.

Ancient Chinese Technology

According to Chinese tradition, the four great inventions of ancient China are the compass, gunpowder, paper, and printing, but there are many more. The Chinese origins of many inventions were forgotten in the period of great scientific and technological development in the West in the seventeenth to twentieth centuries, but we should not forget that these

developments would not have been possible without such commonplace inventions as the horse harness and the plow, both of which probably became known in the West through contact with China in ancient times. When we look at the story of scientific invention we should not see it as a competition between East and West to decide who discovered what first, but as a process of partnership in the building of world civilization—a partnership that continues today.

A *Luopan,* or *Feng Shui* compass, is a key tool in the practice of *Feng Shui*. Each of the eight main points of the compass is assigned a trigram, plus a large number of symbols that can be interpreted according to complex formulas.

Glossary of Names

Bi Sheng inventor, during the Song Dynasty, of the first printing system using movable type

Cai Lun court official during the Han Dynasty who is said to have invented paper

Chi You war god in Chinese mythology who fought Huang Di (the Yellow Emperor)

Dezong Tang Emperor who commissioned Jia Dan to produce a map of China and part of Central Asia

Du Shi government official and engineer during the Han Dynasty whose invention of waterwheel-powered bellows transformed iron-making technology

Guo Shoujing astronomer, engineer, and mathematician during the Yuan Dynasty

Hua Tuo famous physician during the Han Dynasty and Three Kingdoms era, recorded as being the first person to use anesthesia during surgery

Huang Di (Yellow Emperor) legendary Chinese emperor and father of traditional Chinese medicine

Jia Dan Tang Dynasty official, scholar, geographer, and mapmaker, commissioned by Emperor Dezong to produce a map of China and part of Central Asia

Ko Yu Daoist priest who is credited with inventing the wheelbarrow

Kublai Khan fifth and last ruler of the Mongol Empire and who founded the Yuan Dynasty

Lady Dai (Xin Zhui) wife of the Marquis of Dai and member of the aristocracy during the Han Dynasty

Leizu (Xi Lingshi) legendary Chinese empress and wife of the Yellow Emperor, traditionally believed to have discovered silk and to have invented the silk loom

Liu Bang (Emperor Gaozu) former peasant who was founder of the Han Dynasty

Marco Polo Venetian explorer and traveler famous for his journeys across Eurasia, especially along the Silk Road to China during the reign of Kublai Khan

Marquis of Dai member of the aristocracy, or elite upper class, during the Han Dynasty

Mi Huangfu Qin Dynasty physician whose twelve-volume work on acupuncture and moxibustion is still considered very important and influential

Pei Xiu government minister, geographer, and mapmaker who lived during the period of disunity between the Han and Sui dynasties

Qiao Weiyo engineer and government official during the Song Dynasty who invented the pound lock, a system still used on canals and rivers today

Shen Kuo scientist and government official in charge of the Bureau of Astronomy during the Song Dynasty, known for his discovery of true north and calculating the difference between true north and magnetic north

Shen Nong legendary figure in Chinese mythology known as the "Divine Farmer," believed to have given the gifts of agricultural knowledge and herbal medicine

Shi Huangdi, First Emperor Qin founder and first ruler of the Qin Dynasty, which unified China for the first time

Su Song highly respected Song Dynasty scholar in many fields, including zoology, botany, astronomy, chemistry, mapmaking, and clockmaking; also an engineer, politician, poet, and ambassador

Taizu founder and first emperor of the Song Dynasty

Tao Hongjing government official who studied drugs, medicines, and their effects; he also edited and expanded an earlier work on herbal medicine

Wang Anshi economist, politician, and poet of the Song Dynasty who introduced social, economic, and administrative reforms, including examinations for the military, medicine, and the law

Wang Weiyi famous doctor and expert in acupuncture during the Song Dynasty

Wei Boyang author and alchemist of the Han Dynasty who wrote down the first recipe for a substance that was like gunpowder

Wendi founder of the Sui Dynasty

Wu Deren engineer responsible for building a south-pointing carriage

Xuanzang Chinese Buddhist monk, scholar, traveler, and translator during the Tang Dynasty

Yangdi second ruler of Sui Dynasty who was responsible for a huge building program including the completion of the Great Canal, the rebuilding of the Great Wall, and the construction of roads, palaces, and ships

Yixing astronomer, mathematician, engineer, and Buddhist monk during the Tang Dynasty

Yongle third ruler of the Ming Dynasty, considered among China's greatest emperors; he moved China's capital from Nanjing to Beijing, and built the Forbidden City

Zeng Gongliang important scholar during the Song Dynasty; co-author of the first book to record the use of a magnetic compass and gunpowder

Zhang Heng scientist, mathematician, mapmaker, and poet during the Han Dynasty who invented the first seismograph, improved calculations in the formula for pi, developed ways to make maps more accurate, and extensively catalogued the stars

Zhang Sixun astronomer and military engineer during the early Song Dynasty

Zhang Zhongjing famous physician who made valuable contributions to herbal medicine and treating disease, artificial respiration, and fluid replacement

Zheng He explorer, traveler, diplomat, and admiral during the Ming Dynasty who led several maritime expeditions

Glossary

Acupuncture traditional Chinese medicine where very fine, sharp needles are inserted just below the surface of the skin, at specific points or pathways along the body, to improve the body's flow of *qi* (life energy), treat a wide range of illnesses and health problems, or relieve pain

Alchemist person practicing alchemy, the attempt to turn ordinary metals into gold, and to find the secret of eternal life

Anesthesia the giving of drugs so that a person is unconscious or an area of the body is completely numb

Angina spasms of pain in the chest caused by a lack of oxygen flowing to the heart muscles

Artificial respiration the manual or mechanical forcing of air, in a regular rhythm, in and out of the lungs of a person who has stopped breathing on their own

Astrology foretelling of the future through interpretation of the positions and movements of the stars, planets, sun, and moon

Astronomy scientific study of the stars, planets, and the wider universe

Bureaucracy administration of government through fixed rules and procedures, and organized into various departments and offices staffed with officials at varying levels of authority

Cocoon envelope or casing an insect forms around itself while maturing into its adult form

Daoism (also spelled Taoism) system of religion or philosophy focused on the "path" or "way," which emphasizes the need for harmony between humans and nature, living a simple life, and compassion, moderation, and humility

Dynasty succession or series of rulers from the same family

Epidemic rapid spread of an infectious disease among a large number of people in a community or population

Flax a plant grown for its fibers, which are used to make linen cloth and thread, while the seed pods are used for linseed oil

Gynecologist doctor who specializes in the treatment and care of women, particularly in relation to their reproductive systems

Inflation continual rise in the general price for goods and services over time, so that more money is needed to buy the same amount

Lodestone naturally occurring piece of the mineral magnetite that has magnetic properties

Meridian in acupuncture, any of the pathways along which *qi*, or energy, flows throughout the body

Metronome clock-like mechanical instrument used to mark tempo in music by ticking at precise and equal intervals

Moxa dried and crushed mugwort (*Artemisia vulgaris*) used in the practice of moxibustion

Moxibustion traditional Chinese medicine practice where lit moxa sticks are placed on specific areas and acupuncture points on the body, to stimulate circulation and promote the flow of *qi*

Nomadic traveling and moving from place to place, without a permanent home, but usually following a seasonal pattern

Odometer instrument for measuring distance traveled

Ophthalmologist doctor who specializes in treatment and care of the eyes

Pediatrician doctor who specializes in treatment and care of babies and children

Pendulum a weighted rod suspended or balanced from a fixed point, so that it moves back and forth under the influence of gravity; used to regulate a clock

Prefect high government official put in charge of a region or city

Pupa (pl. pupae) middle stage in the life of an insect when it is wrapped in a cocoon, between its immature and adult forms

Saltpeter potassium nitrate or sodium nitrate; salt made from the alkali metals potassium or sodium, and used in gunpowder and explosives, fireworks, fertilizers, and to preserve or cure meat

Seismograph instrument designed to detect and measure vibrations within the earth, particularly tremors and earthquakes

Sericulture raising of silkworms to make silk

Stele (pl. stelae) stone or slab that stands upright with an inscribed or sculptured surface; used as a monument or commemorative tablet

Taiqiquan ancient exercise system of slow, smoothly flowing movements designed to relax the body and the mind; originally developed as a martial art, it is still hugely popular and widely practiced for exercise and as a type of meditation

Tumor abnormal growth of tissue in the body

Yang male aspect of the universal energy or life force (*qi*); represented by light, heat, and dryness

Yin feminine aspect of the universal energy or life force (*qi*); represented by darkness, coolness, and wetness

Learn More About

Books

Beshore, George. *Science in Ancient China (Science of the Past).* New York: Franklin Watts, 1998

Cotterell, Arthur & Buller, Laura. *Ancient China (DK Eyewitness Books).* New York: Dorling Kindersley, 2005

Ebrey, Patricia B. *The Cambridge Illustrated History of China (Cambridge Illustrated Histories).* New York: Cambridge University Press, 1999

Greenberger, Robert. *The Technology of Ancient China (The Technology of the Ancient World).* New York: Rosen Central, 2006

Hollihan-Elliot, Sheila. *Ancient History Of China (History and Culture of China).* Broomall, PA: Mason Crest Publishers, 2005

Kramer, Lance. *Great Ancient China Projects You Can Build Yourself (Build It Yourself).* White River Junction, VT: Nomad Press, 2008

Nicholson R. & Watts C. *Ancient China (Journey Into Civilization).* New York: Chelsea House Publications, 1994

Portal, Jane. *The First Emperor: China's Terracotta Army.* Cambridge, Mass: Harvard University Press, 2007

Temple, Robert. *The Genius of China: 3,000 Years of Science, Discovery, and Invention.* Rochester, VT: Inner Traditions, 2007

Williams, Suzanne. *Made in China: Ideas and Inventions from Ancient China.* Berkeley, CA: Pacific View Press, 1997

Web Sites

About.com—Chinese inventions
http://inventors.about.com/od/chineseinventors/Chinese_Inventions.htm

Baltimore County Public Schools—China Dynasties and Contributions
www.bcps.org/offices/lis/models/chinahist/dynasties.html

The British Museum—Ancient China
www.ancientchina.co.uk

The British Museum—Early Imperial China
www.earlyimperialchina.co.uk

ChinaCulture.org—Created in China
www.chinaculture.org/gb/en_madeinchina/node_2498.htm

CNN—China Inventions Timeline
http://www.cnn.com/interactive/specials/9908/china.inventions.timeline/frameset.exclude.html

Computersmiths—History of Chinese Invention and Discovery
www.computersmiths.com/chineseinvention/

Oracle—Thinkquest — Ancient Chinese Technology
http://library.thinkquest.org/23062/

San Diego County Office of Education—Medieval Chinese Inventions and Innovations
www.sdcoe.k12.ca.us/score/chinin/chinintg.htm

Index